AN
ODYSSEY
INTO
GREEK
COOKING

JUNE MARINOS

AN
ODYSSEY
INTO
GREEK
COOKING

TERZOPOULOS BOOKS

June Marinos

June Marinos was born in London of Welsh and Irish parentage, and is married to a Greek economist and World War II veteran whom she met in Bulgaria. She has three children, one of whom successfully runs a beach salad bar and an Indian restaurant on the island of Zakynthos. During World War II she served in the Women's Royal Naval Service and worked in the Orkneys and Egypt. After the end of the war she joined the Foreign Office and served in Bulgaria and Luxembourg. Since 1951 she has been living in Greece, except for several years spent abroad in Thailand, Iran, Ethiopia and Zaire. She has travelled widely in Europe, Africa, the Far East and North America. As well as writing a cookery column for the Chandris Hotels magazine, she has published a booklet about Zakynthos cooking, has completed a draft of a book with some 160 ways of cooking eggplant, and is currently working on a book of Ionian Island cookery.

Text Editor: Barbara Terzopoulos
Picture Stylist: Simone Cafiri
Photographers: Alexandra Klein and Yannis Kalogridis: Studio Imago

ISBN 960-7220-20-X

Contents

Prologue

From an early age I was always interested in food and travel. One of my earliest recollections was a trip with my parents to France during which I kept a notebook with a list of what I ate for every meal! My first attempt at cooking was when I was about five years old and fried pieces of potato on top of a coke boiler until they turned black!

In 1951, I arrived in Greece by boat from Bari to "spy out the land", as my father put it, before I married my Greek fiancé. After a short stay in Athens I was swept off to the Ionian island of Zakynthos, which I found a paradise. My future mother-in-law approved of me, so we were married on the island and came to live in Athens. It was not long before I developed a great interest in Greek cookery. My landlady taught me many of its mysteries but I had to learn the hard way — cooking on a parafin stove and drawing water from a well. This made cooking a lengthy process. After that, everywhere I travelled in Greece I asked questions about local cooking, started collecting recipes, and made plans in my mind to write a cookery book one day.

I spent about ten years out of Greece but during that time I had many Greek friends (especially in Ethiopia) who gave me recipes. Eventually when I returned to Greece I decided to try to write a cookery book with different eggplant recipes from all over the world. I became involved with the International Women's Club in Athens, and at one point gave courses of Greek cookery lessons together with some other friends, and on my own. Later on, a friend heard about my book on eggplant and asked me if I would write an article about the vegetable for the Chandris Hotels Magazine. Consequently I became a regular contributor of articles on Greek food. I then decided to write a small booklet on the food of Zakynthos. My interests became more involved with Greek cuisine, and so I undertook to write this book.

I love Greek food and miss it when I go abroad. It is simple, down to earth, satisfying and contains many vegetables, salads and fruit. Traditionally very little or no butter is used, only olive oil. Many complete meals can be cooked in one saucepan or one baking dish, and taste good when re-heated. In Greece one must always be prepared for extra relations or friends at meals. Family members often eat at different times, so this type of food is the ideal answer. Many of the dishes can be prepared early in the morning and re-heated or eaten at room temperature.

In many ways Greek cuisine resembles southern Italian cuisine, only the Greeks prefer lamb to veal, and do not use salted bacon in their cooking. In general the Greeks are great pasta eaters; in fact, they are reputed to eat more pasta than the Italians — although they prepare it rather differently. The cooking of the Ionian Islands resembles Italian cuisine even more in that they use a lot of tomatoes, garlic and pasta. Other similarities are found, for example, in the national dish of Zákynthos called "sáltsa", which is a beef ragôut containing pieces of cheese. The air-dried pork smothered in black peppercorns, bay leaves and garlic reminds one of a primitive form of proscuitto, and the Christmas bread, "Christopsoma" is much like pannetone.

One of the main differences between French and Greek cooking is that traditionally the Greeks do not use cream in their cooking, and rarely use butter. However, nowadays that cream is more widely available it is used more often. The current generation is much less conservative about their cooking habits than older generations. In Greek cooking, quantities are not as precise as in many French recipes and, in general, no difficult techniques are required. A beautiful puffed-up French soufflé would be difficult to serve for a dinner party in Greece as Greeks are not renowned for their punctuality! Generally speaking, the Greeks do not like their meat underdone, but they are not particular about their food being piping hot or about warmed plates.

One can find many similarities to the cooking of Provence. The famous bouillabaisse is a Mediterranean speciality. Connoisseurs consider that the authentic bouillabaisse is made only in the region between Marseilles and Toulon. Venus is said to have invented this dish, but others attribute it to an abbess of a Marseilles convent. As Marseilles was once an ancient Greek colony, perhaps it originated from "kakaviá", the Greek fish soup often made by fishermen with the unsold remains of their catch. It is a simple form of bouillabaisse. The French of Provence, like the Greeks, love salt cod and eat it with aioli whilst the Greeks eat it with skordaliá, but the essential ingredient in both is garlic. A great delicacy in Greece is a dried and pressed grey mullet roe called "avgotarako", most of which is produced in Messolónghi. In the Marseilles area, poutargue is produced, which is more or less the same. This is one of the most ancient of food products, known to the Cretans in the time of King Minos. It was imported to Provence as early as 6th century B.C., by Greek seamen from the area of Fokidha.

One of the main differences between Greek and Middle Eastern cuisine is in the use of spices. The Greeks use only cloves, nutmeg, cumin, cinnamon, allspice and black pepper. Red pepper is mainly used in northern Greece and Corfu. Cooks in the Middle East use ginger, cardamon, saffron (which was used in ancient Greece), tumeric, coriander (seeds and fresh), caraway, aniseed, fenugreek, mastic, mahlab and sumac. Tahini, a paste made from crashed sesame seeds, is used for quite a few Middle Eastern dishes whilst in Greece is it only used to make a soup for Lent. There are also similarities between the cuisines. Phýllo pastry is used throughout the Middle East as it is in Greece, to make pies small, large, savoury and sweet. Baklavá, kataífi, ekmék and galactobúreko are a few of the well known sweets common in both areas.

Greek food is modern and healthy. Desserts are eaten only on special occasions and fruit nearly always follows the main course. Salads are consumed at every meal, as are boiled greens, either cultivated or wild, topped with olive oil and lemon juice — all alive with vitamins! Wine is drunk in moderation and alchoholic drinks are almost always accompanied by a mezé (appetizer), with the result that one rarely sees a drunken Greek.

Nowadays Greek food does not swim in olive oil as it used to. People are more conscious of their weight and have adapted the Greek cuisine to this purpose. Pasta of wholewheat, brown rice, brown flour, light cheese, skimmed milk, yoghurt, low calorie jams and even ham are widely available. A slogan for the 21st century could be eat Greek and stay healthy!

Salads &
Hors D'Oeuvres

Greek Salad

Χωριάτικη Σαλάτα

Greek salad (in Greek, called "village" or "peasant salad"), is by far the most popular. Its success depends upon your using the best-tasting tomatoes available. As a rule, Greek salad is served with taverna meals whenever tomatoes are in season. The necessary ingredients are the cucumber, tomato, féta cheese and olive oil; all other elements of the salad are optional. Lettuce of any kind is an unusual addition to this salad in Greece, though it is often included abroad. A Greek salad suffices for a light summer meal.

3 firm tomatoes, cut in eighths
1 cucumber, peeled and sliced
½ green pepper, seeded and thinly sliced lengthwise
1 medium-sized onion, thinly sliced
100 g (1 cup) cubed féta cheese
75 g (½ cup) black Kalamáta or other ripe olives
½ tsp oregano
Salt
3 tbsp olive oil
1 tbsp vinegar
2 tbsp capers (optional)

Combine all the ingredients and serve the salad immediately.
Variation: Add slices of avocado or carrot.

Serves 6

Fáva

Φάβα

The proper way to eat fáva is to break off a chunk of fresh bread and using a butter knife, spread the fáva thickly on the bread. Top it with a slice of an onion, a squeeze of lemon, and a sprinkling of red pepper. Yellow split peas make a more attractive dish than the green ones, and they say the best yellow split peas come from the island of Santorini.

500 g (1 lb) yellow or green split peas
1 large onion, plus a few onion slices for garnishing
4 tbsp olive oil
Salt and freshly ground black pepper
Cayenne pepper
Lemon wedges for garnishing

Cover the split peas with unsalted water. Boil them together with the whole onion and half of the olive oil until the peas are tender and the water has evaporated, about 30 to 40 minutes.

Mash the peas, sieve them, or purée in a food processor. The fáva should be a bit thicker than mashed potatoes. Season with salt and pepper.

Spread the fáva on a serving dish, sprinkle with the remaining olive oil, the cayenne pepper, and garnish with slices of raw onion and lemon wedges. Serve with fresh bread and black olives.

Serves 6

Mykonian Black-Eyed Pea Salad
Μαυρομάτικα Φασόλια Σαλάτα

These small, dried black-eyed peas are available at Greek or Italian specialty shops. The salad may be prepared ahead of time as it keeps well in the refrigerator for several days. Just remove it an hour before serving so the oil liquifies. A little chopped tomato and parsley added at the last moment make the dish more colorful.

250 g (2 cups) black-eyed peas
2 garlic cloves, finely chopped
4 green onions, finely chopped
6 cl (¼) cup olive oil
2 tbsp vinegar
Salt and freshly ground black pepper

Boil the peas in unsalted water for 30 to 40 minutes, or until just tender. Drain and place them in a bowl.
Heat the olive oil in a skillet and sauté the garlic and green onions for 3 to 4 minutes. Add the vinegar, stir, and pour this dressing over the black-eyed peas, mixing well. Season with salt and pepper. Serve cold.
Serves 4 to 6

Butter Bean Salad
Γίγαντες Σαλάτα

250 g (8 oz) large dried butter beans, soaked overnight in cold water
2 tbsp chopped celery leaves
2 green onions, chopped
1 tbsp finely chopped parsley
1 lemon, juice only
8 cl (6 tbsp) olive oil
Salt and freshly ground black pepper

Drain, rinse, then boil the beans in unsalted water for 1½ hours, or until soft. Drain the beans and plunge them immediately into cold water to prevent their splitting. Drain again when ready to use.
In a large bowl, combine the beans with all the ingredients, adding salt and pepper to taste. Refrigerate for several hours before serving.
Serves 6

Lentil Salad
Φακές Σαλάτα

250 g (8 oz) lentils
2 bay leaves
1 tsp oregano
2 garlic cloves, finely chopped
Salt and freshly ground black pepper
3 tbsp olive oil
1 tbsp vinegar

In a saucepan, cover the lentils and bay leaves with cold unsalted water. Bring to the boil and simmer for 30 minutes, or until the lentils are just tender. Drain them and rinse lightly in cold water. In a bowl combine the lentils with the remaining ingredients and mix well. Chill and serve.
Serves 6

Traditional Eggplant Salad

Χωριάτικη Μελιτζανοσαλάτα

1 kg (2 lb) large eggplant
2 tbsp finely chopped parsley
3 garlic cloves, finely chopped
12 cl (½ cup) olive oil
6 cl (¼ cup) vinegar
Salt and freshly ground black pepper

Prick the eggplant well with a fork and bake in an oven preheated to 220°C (425°F) for 30 minutes, or until tender. Cut in half and discarding any tough seedy parts, scoop out the flesh. Chop the flesh and combine it in a bowl with the remaining ingredients.
Serve with fresh bread.
Variation: Add some finely chopped green pepper, or grill the eggplant over direct heat, as described in the following recipe.
Serves 10 to 12

Modern Eggplant Salad

Μοντέρνα Μελιτζανοσαλάτα

This eggplant salad is particularly appetizing when served as a dip because it has a creamy consistency and a delicate green color.

2 medium-sized eggplant
2 lemons, juice only
12 cl (½ cup) olive oil
4 tbsp vinegar
2 tsp Dijon mustard
50 g (1 cup) finely chopped parsley
1 egg yolk
Salt and freshly ground black pepper

Prepare the eggplant as below. After rinsing, put the eggplant in a colander, pour over the lemon juice, and let them drain for one hour to eliminate the excess liquid.
Combine all the ingredients except the egg yolk in a blender or food processor, and process for one minute. Add the egg yolk and process a few seconds more. Add salt and pepper to taste.
Serves 8

PREPARING THE EGGPLANT

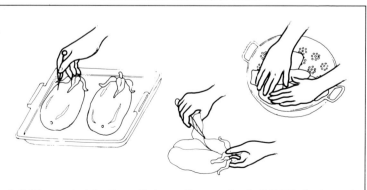

1. Grill the eggplant directly over the burner. Turn occasionally. **2.** Hold by the stem and peel upwards. **3.** Rinse lightly and drain in a colander. Squeeze out excess moisture.

Special Eggplant Salad

Μελιτζανοσαλάτα

Omit the olive oil and yogurt, be sparing with the salt, and you will have a delicious low calorie dish.

1 kg (2 lb) large eggplant
2 tbsp finely chopped cucumber
2 tbsp peeled, seeded and finely chopped tomato
2 tbsp finely chopped green pepper
1 tbsp finely chopped parsley
1 tbsp finely chopped onion
1 garlic clove, finely chopped
6 tbsp olive oil
3 tbsp vinegar
225 g (1 cup) thick yogurt, mayonnaise, or sour cream
Salt and freshly ground black pepper
Cayenne pepper

Prick the eggplant well with a fork and grill directly over a gas flame, electric burner or charcoal for 20 minutes, or until the skin is charred and the flesh is tender. This will give the eggplant a smoky flavor.
While still hot, hold them by the stem and remove all the charred skin, peeling from the bottom up toward the stem. Rinse lightly under cold water and squeeze out excess moisture.
Put the eggplant in a bowl and mash with a fork. Add all the other ingredients and mix. Season with salt, pepper and cayenne pepper to taste.
Serves 10 to 12

Syros Caper Dip

Συριανή Καπαροσαλάτα

Capers grow wild all over Greece, especially in the Cycladic Islands.

200 g (1 cup) capers, drained and well washed
2 egg yolks
1 medium-sized potato, quartered and freshly boiled
1 tsp prepared mustard
Salt and freshly ground pepper
35 cl (1½ cups) olive oil
1 tbsp lemon juice

Combine the capers, egg yolks, potato and mustard in a blender or food processor and purée until smooth. Add the olive oil in a stream, then the lemon juice. Season with salt and pepper. Serve as a dip with raw carrots, cauliflower or small pieces of fresh bread.
Variation: In place of the capers you may substitute 50 g (one firmly packed cup) of chopped parsley, celery, dill or mint.
Serves 6

Tzatzíki

Τζατζίκι

A universal favorite, tzatzíki goes with everything. It is often served as a dip for fresh bread, or with fried eggplant and zucchini slices, with souvláki, or with roast lamb or chicken. The most important ingredient in tzatzíki is the yogurt. Buy the thickest yogurt you can find, or thicken your own. Strain 900 g (4 cups) of yogurt overnight in a cheese cloth bag. The water will drain off and reduce the yogurt to about half its volume, leaving it with a wonderfully thick consistency.

450 g (2 cups) Greek strained yogurt
½ cucumber, peeled and finely chopped or grated
1 tbsp finely chopped fresh mint (optional)
2 or 3 garlic cloves, finely chopped
1 tbsp olive oil
Salt and freshly ground black pepper

Combine all the ingredients and season to taste. Refrigerate for several hours to blend the flavors.
Serves 6 to 8

Walnut Garlic Dip

Σκορδαλιά με Καρύδια

This is delicious served with fried zucchini or eggplant, boiled beets or fish. It is also an interesting dip for raw vegetables.

100 g (1 cup) walnuts
4 or 5 garlic cloves
100 g (1 cup) breadcrumbs, soaked in water and squeezed
¼ liter (1 cup) olive oil
2 tbsp vinegar or lemon juice
Salt and freshly ground black pepper

Process the walnuts and garlic in a blender for a few seconds. Add the breadcrumbs and process again. Then add the olive oil and vinegar or lemon juice and process once more. Season with salt and pepper.
Serves 6 to 8

Romaine Lettuce Salad

Μαρούλι Σαλάτα

Salads are by and large seasonal in Greece. Romaine lettuce is abundant during the spring and fall. During the coldest months of winter, cabbage salad is popular, and during the hottest months of summer, luscious red tomatoes are standard fare. For the most delicate salad, use only the heart and tender pale green leaves of the romaine lettuce. Reserve the dark, tough, outer leaves for garnishing other dishes.

1 large romaine lettuce, washed, dried and thinly sliced crosswise
3 tbsp olive oil
2 tbsp finely chopped green onions
2 tbsp finely chopped dill
1 tbsp vinegar
Salt and freshly ground black pepper

Place the lettuce in a salad bowl and toss it with the olive oil. Combine the remaining ingredients, add them to the salad, and toss again.
Serves 4 to 6

Cabbage Salad

Λαχανοσαλάτα

Cabbages grow to enormous size in Greece, but a small firm head gives best results for salad.

1 small white cabbage, finely sliced
2 carrots, grated
3 celery sticks, finely chopped
1 green pepper, finely sliced
3 tbsp olive oil
1 lemon, juice only
Salt and freshly ground black pepper

Combine all the ingredients, mix well and serve.
Serves 6 to 8

Red Cabbage Salad

Κόκκινο Λάχανο Σαλάτα

The sweet-sour flavor of this salad is intriguing. It compliments ham, pork or game particularly well.

1 medium-sized red cabbage, grated
1 tart apple, grated
2 tbsp horseradish sauce
2 tsp Dijon mustard
4 tbsp sugar
6 cl (¼ cup) olive oil
Salt and freshly ground black pepper
2 tbsp vinegar

Combine all the ingredients in a bowl. Let the flavors mingle for at least one hour before serving.
Serves 6

Skordaliá

Σκορδαλιά

As the garlic flavor is not subtle in skordaliá, and its aroma tends to linger, serve only to garlic lovers.

6 large garlic cloves
3 medium-sized waxy potatoes, boiled, peeled and quartered
1 lemon, juice strained
12 cl (½ cup) water or fish stock
Salt
2 tbsp olive oil

This sauce is traditionally made in a mortar and pestle. Pound the garlic to a paste. Add the warm potatoes and pound vigorously to a stiff paste. Add the lemon juice and water, or fish stock, and pound again. The sauce should be very gooey. Add salt to taste.
Transfer the skordaliá to a serving dish and let the flavors mingle for one hour before serving topped with the olive oil.
You may also make skordaliá in a food processor or blender. Process the garlic for a few seconds. Add the warm potatoes and the water or fish stock and process again. Add the lemon juice and salt; process once more. Serve topped with olive oil.

Serves 6 to 8

Taramosaláta with Bread

Ταραμοσαλάτα με Ψωμί

2 tbsp taramá (salted cod's roe)
¼ liter (1 cup) olive oil
8 cl (⅓ cup) lemon juice
250 g (8 oz) day-old white
bread, crusts removed, soaked in water and well squeezed

Put all the ingredients in the food processor or blender, and process for one minute. Stir and if necessary, process longer until the taramá is completely blended. Serve with fresh bread.

Serves 10 to 12

Taramosaláta with Potato

Ταραμοσαλάτα με Πατάτα

1 tbsp taramá (salted cod's roe)
3 medium-sized waxy potatoes, boiled, peeled and quartered
12 cl (½ cup) olive oil
2 lemons, juice only
2 tbsp finely chopped green onions
2 tbsp finely chopped parsley
1 tbsp finely chopped dill
Salt

Process the potatoes until smooth; add the taramá and process again. With the processor on, add the olive oil and lemon juice alternately. Add the herbs last. Add salt and if necessary, more lemon juice to taste.

Serves 8

17

Chestnut and Walnut Terrine

Πατέ από Κάστανα και Καρύδια

This is an excellent vegetarian dish for Christmas Day.

500 g (1 lb) chestnuts, boiled, skinned and chopped (reserve
several whole for decoration)
3 tbsp finely chopped walnuts (plus several whole for decoration)
4 green onions, finely chopped
1 garlic clove, finely chopped
6 celery sticks, finely chopped
175 g (1½ cups) whole wheat breadcrumbs
60 g (4 tbsp) butter
3 tbsp grated Gruyère cheese
4 tbsp Mavrodáphne wine (or other sweet red wine)
2 eggs, slightly beaten
Salt and freshly ground black pepper
1 to 3 tbsp milk, if necessary
3 bay leaves
Romaine lettuce to garnish

Sauté the green onions and garlic in the butter until transparent. Blend
or process the chestnuts and walnuts to a purée. Combine these and all
the other ingredients, except the bay leaves, in a bowl and mix well.
Add a little milk if necessary, so that the mixture has the consistency of
mashed potato.
Line a buttered oblong terrine about 30 by 12 cm (12 by 5 in) with buttered waxed paper. Transfer the mixture to the terrine, pressing down
well; smooth the top with a knife. Decorate with the whole chestnuts,
walnuts and bay leaves. Cover with buttered waxed paper.
Place the tin on a rack in a hot water bath (bain marie). Cook in a moderate oven preheated to 180°C (350°F), for one hour.
Cool the terrine, remove the greaseproof paper from the top, and carefully lift out onto a serving dish. Surround with finely shredded romaine
lettuce.
Serves 12 to 14

Smoked Trout Mousse Loredana

Μους από Καπνιστή Πέστροφα

Fresh trout are raised commercially in the rivers of northern Greece. Just out-side the cities of Naoussa and Ioannina, one can select his own trout from pools in the river, and have it cooked to order. Serve this mousse as a first course for a formal dinner, or with a Greek salad for lunch.

250 g (½ lb) smoked trout, lightly mashed
14 g (½ oz) powdered gelatine
4 tbsp (¼ cup) cold water
½ liter (2 cups) fresh cream
12 cl (1 cup) mayonnaise (see inside cover)
1 small onion, very finely grated
2 tbsp very finely chopped parsley
2 tbsp lemon juice
Salt

Sprinkle the gelatine on top of the cold water and leave for five minutes. Put 4 tbsp of the cream in a small saucepan, add the gelatine and water, and heat until the gelatine is dissolved. Set the mixture aside to cool slightly.
In a bowl, beat the remaining cream until fairly stiff. Stir in the gelatine mixture, then add the remaining ingredients. Season with salt to taste.
Pour into an oiled ring mold and refrigerate for 24 hours.
Turn out the mousse and decorate it with parsley, slices of lemon and ripe olives. Fill the center with finely shredded lettuce.
Serves 8

Artichoke Mousse Marinos

Αγκινάρες Μους

This is a deliciously rich first course, or an elegant main dish for a summer luncheon. Local ingredients provide the inspiration for this recipe as well as for the preceeding one, smoked trout mousse.

5 or 6 artichoke hearts (fresh, frozen or tinned)
14 g (½ oz) powdered gelatine
¼ liter (1 cup) cold chicken stock, or 1 chicken bouillon cube
dissolved in ¼ liter (1 cup) water
½ liter (2 cups) fresh cream
12 cl (½ cup) mayonnaise
4 tbsp chopped fresh dill or parsley
2 tbsp Mavrodaphne wine (or other sweet red wine)
1 tbsp lemon juice
Salt and pepper

If using either fresh or frozen artichoke hearts, boil them in salted water with the juice of one lemon until tender. Mash them and set aside.

In a saucepan, sprinkle the gelatine on the chicken stock, soak it for five minutes, then heat and stir until the gelatine has dissolved. Transfer to a bowl and refrigerate for 20 minutes, or until almost set. Whip the cream until stiff, stir it into the gelatine mixture, then add all the other ingredients. Season if necessary.

Pour the mousse into an oiled 20 cm (8 in) ring mold and refrigerate for 24 hours. Dip the mold in very hot water for 10 seconds, then turn out the mousse onto a serving dish. Surround it with shredded lettuce and decorate with finely sliced cucumber and springs of fresh dill.

Serves 6

Eggplant Pickles

Μελιτζάνες Τουρσί

Use the small slim eggplant for this "toursí", or pickle. Look for ones that are absolutely purple, with no white streaks. If available, use the Mediterranean variety of celery, which has a thinner stem and is easier to wrap around the stuffed eggplant. Serve the pickles with drinks and a selection of other mezés.

3 kg (6 lb) slim purple eggplant, 7 to 10 cm (3 to 4 in) long
¾ liter (3 cups) vinegar, plus enough vinegar to cover the pickles
1 head of celery, sticks and leaves
3 or 4 hot peppers, finely chopped
3 or 4 garlic cloves, thinly sliced
Salt
Olive oil

Make a lengthwise incision in each eggplant, being careful not to break the skin on the other side. Boil the eggplant in salted water and ¼ liter (one cup) vinegar for 20 minutes, until just tender. Drain well.

In another saucepan, simmer the celery sticks until tender. Chop the celery leaves and mix with the peppers and garlic. Stuff the incisions of the eggplant with 1 tsp of the mixture. Wrap several strands of celery sticks around each eggplant to keep the stuffing in.

Transfer the eggplant to a deep ceramic dish, and cover them with the remaining vinegar. Let marinate for 12 hours, then drain. Transfer the eggplant to sterilized jars, and fill to the top with olive oil.

Green Pepper Salad

Πιπεροσαλάτα

Serve green pepper salad with an assortment of mezés, or together with a main course. Keeps well for several days in the refrigerator.

1 kg (2 lb) green peppers, cut in lengthwise strips
6 tbsp olive oil
3 medium-sized tomatoes, halved, seeded and grated, skins discarded
3 tbsp finely chopped parsley
4 or 5 garlic cloves, finely chopped
¼ tsp sugar
Salt and freshly ground black pepper

Sauté the peppers in the olive oil until soft and slightly browned. Add the tomatoes, parsley and garlic; season with salt, pepper and sugar. Simmer about 20 minutes, or until the sauce thickens.
Serve warm or cold.
Serves 8

Sautéed Peppers

Τσιγαριστές Πιπεριές

Use the long slim Mediterranean peppers for this dish. It is quick and easy to prepare and tastes wonderful.

500 g (1 lb) small green peppers with stalks left on
6 tbsp olive oil
Salt
3 tbsp vinegar

Sauté the peppers in 2 tbsp of the olive oil until soft and slightly browned. Transfer them to a serving dish, season with salt, and pour over the remaining oil and the vinegar. Serve warm or at room temperature.
Serves 6 to 8

Eggs in Tomato Sauce

Αυγά Στραπατσάδα

A popular dish in the Ionian Islands, strapatsáda varies from family to family as well as from island to island. In Kephalonia, I have eaten it cold as a mezé. In Zakynthos, garlic is a common ingredient in the sauce, and the eggs are left to cook whole. In Corfu, dried oregano, thyme or chopped fresh basil are often added. These glorified scrambled eggs are never served at breakfast!

8 eggs
4 large tomatoes, halved, seeded and grated, skins discarded
4 tbsp olive oil
Salt and freshly ground black pepper
½ tsp sugar

Heat the oil in a large frying pan. In it simmer the tomatoes, seasoned with salt, pepper and sugar, until the oil and the tomato separate.
Break the eggs into a bowl and pour them over the tomatoes. Mix well and cook gently over low heat until the liquid evaporates.
Correct the seasoning if necessary, and serve hot with fried potatoes.
Serves 4 to 5

Deep-Fried Zucchini and Eggplant

Τηγανητά Κολοκυθάκια και Μελιτζάνες

*Zucchini is really the star of this dish. Make an effort to keep the fried vege-
tables warm in the oven as you cook the remaining slices, as the hotter and
crispier they are, the better. Serve the fried zucchini and eggplant with a cool
tzatzíki; the contrast is marvelous.*

250 g (½ lb) zucchini, thinly sliced lengthwise
1 medium-sized eggplant, thinly sliced lengthwise
2 egg whites, lightly beaten
Flour
Salt
Corn or sunflower seed oil for deep frying

Sprinkle the zucchini with salt and leave the slices to drain in a colander
for about two hours. Place the eggplant in salted water, leave it for one
hour, then drain in a colander for one hour.
Put about 1 cup of flour in each of 2 bowls. Dip each slice in the first
bowl of flour, shake off excess, then dip in the egg whites. Coat with the
flour in the second bowl.
Deep fry the slices three or four at a time, until golden and crispy. Drain
them on absorbent paper and serve hot with tzatzíki, page 14, or
skordaliá, page 7.
Serves 4 to 6

Zucchini Flower Fritters

Κολοκυθολουλουδοτηγανίτες

The Greek name for these, kolokythólouloudotiganítes, must be one of the longest words in any language. Zucchini is easily grown and extremely popular in Greece, where it is often sold with the flowers fresh and intact. If you cultivate your own, pick the flowers off the end of the zucchini when they are about 3 cm (1½ in) diameter.

100 g (1½ cups) zucchini flowers, with the yellow pistil and
stamens removed
2 tbsp flour
1 egg
1 tbsp water
2 tbsp finely chopped dill or mint
2 tbsp finely chopped green onion or onion
Salt and freshly ground black pepper
Olive oil for sautéing

Wash the zucchini flowers well and chop them finely. Combine the flour, egg and water to make a thick batter, which should have the consistency of thick pancake batter. Add dill or mint, onion and zucchini flowers, and season with salt and pepper. If too thick, add some water; if too thin, add a little flour.

Heat 3 cm (1 in) of olive oil in a skillet and drop in the batter by tablespoonfuls. Sauté gently on both sides until golden. Drain the fritters on paper towels and serve them hot with drinks or chilled white wine.

Serves 6

Santorini Tomato Fritters

Ντοματοκεφτέδες

Santorini is home to its own special variety of tomato, very small and irregularly shaped, and grown with a minimum of water in the volcanic soil of the island. Fresh plum tomatoes are an acceptable substitute.

250 g (2 cups) chopped plum tomatoes
2 slices day-old white bread, crusts removed, soaked in water
and squeezed
2 tbsp finely chopped onion
4 tbsp flour
1 tsp mint, dried or fresh
Pinch baking soda
¼ tsp cinnamon
Salt and freshly ground black pepper
Olive oil for frying

Combine all the ingredients and add a few tablespoons of water if necessary to make a very thick batter. Let rest one hour, then fry the batter by tablespoonfuls in the hot olive oil until golden brown on both sides. Drain well on paper towels and serve with drinks.

Makes 16 fritters

Taramá Croquettes

Ταραμοκεφτέδες

2 tbsp taramá
250 g (8 oz) day-old white bread, crusts removed, soaked in water
and well squeezed
6 tbsp finely chopped dill
2 tbsp finely chopped onion or green onion
1 egg, separated
½ tsp baking powder
2 tsp lemon juice
1 tsp yogurt
Freshly ground black pepper
75 g (½ cup) flour
Oil for deep-frying

Combine all the ingredients except the egg white and flour. Beat the
egg white until stiff and gently fold it into the mixture. Refrigerate for one
hour. Shape the chilled mixture into walnut-size balls. Roll them in flour
and deep-fry. Drain on paper towels and serve hot.

Makes about 20 croquettes

Fried Cauliflower Florets

Τηγανητό Κουνουπίδι

1 medium-sized cauliflower cut into florets, parboiled 5 minutes,
and drained well
Batter
150 g (1 cup) flour
1 tsp baking powder
2 eggs, separated
12 cl (½ cup) milk
1 tbsp olive oil
1 tbsp lemon juice
Nutmeg
Salt and freshly ground black pepper
Mayonnaise Sauce
¼ lit (1 cup) mayonnaise
2 tbsp chopped parsley
1 tbsp chopped capers
1 tbsp vinegar
1 tbsp lemon juice
Pepper

First prepare the batter. Sift the flour and baking powder together. Add
the egg yolks, mix well, then stir in the milk, olive oil, and lemon juice.
Season with salt, pepper and nutmeg. Beat the egg whites until stiff and
add them to the mixture. The batter should be thick.
To prepare the mayonnaise sauce, combine all the ingredients and mix
well.
Dip the florets in the batter and deep-fry in oil until golden brown. Drain
on paper towels and serve with mayonnaise sauce.

Serves 4 to 6

Gígantes with Mayonnaise Sauce

Τηγανητοί Γίγαντες με Μαγιονέζα

250 gr (8 oz) large dried butter beans, soaked overnight in cold
water, rinsed and drained
Flour
12 cl (½ cup) olive oil for sautéing
Mayonnaise Sauce
¼ liter (1 cup) mayonnaise
2 tbsp tomato ketchup
1 tbsp Worcestershire sauce
1 tsp Dijon mustard
Salt and freshly ground black pepper

Boil the beans in unsalted water for 1 to 1½ hours, until just tender.
Drain the beans and plunge them immediately into cold water to pre-
vent their splitting. Drain again, dip in flour and sauté briefly in the olive
oil. Drain on paper towels.
To prepare the sauce, combine all the ingredients and season to taste
with salt and pepper.
Serve the gígantes hot with the mayonnaise sauce in a separate bowl.
Serves 6

Sautéed Chicken Livers

Συκώτι Μεζές

250 g (8 oz) chicken livers, quartered
1 tbsp butter
Salt and freshly ground black pepper
1 tsp oregano
Lemon wedges

Sauté the liver in the butter for about five minutes, or until just done.
Season with salt and pepper, sprinkle with oregano, and garnish with
the lemon wedges. Serve hot.
Serves 6

Mussel Salad

Μύδια Σαλάτα

250 g (8 oz) steamed mussels, fresh or frozen, or tinned mussels
400 g (2 cups) long grain rice, boiled and cooled
150 g (1 cup) finely chopped green olives
2 tbsp finely chopped parsley
1 tbsp finely chopped gherkins, plus several whole ones
1 tbsp chopped pimento
1 tbsp lemon juice
Salt and freshly ground black pepper
¼ liter (1 cup) mayonnaise

Combine all the ingredients and press into a decorative mold. Turn out
and garnish with whole gherkins.
Serves 6

Mushroom Ramekins Marinos

Μανιτάρια Σουφλέ

500 g (1 lb) mushrooms, washed, dried and sliced
1 garlic clove, halved
2 finely chopped green onions
60 g (4 tbsp) butter
2 tbsp brandy
Salt and freshly ground black pepper
4 tbsp finely chopped parsley or dill
4 tbsp finely grated Gruyère cheese
2 tbsp flour
¼ liter (1 cup) milk
1 tbsp Samos wine (or other sweet red or white wine)
1 to 2 tbsp lemon juice
3 tbsp breadcrumbs
Cayenne pepper

Rub 6 ramekin dishes with the cut clove of garlic and butter them well. Sauté the mushrooms and green onions in 1 tbsp butter. When nearly all the liquid has evaporated, add the brandy and simmer until it has evaporated too. Season with salt and pepper. Distribute the mushrooms among the ramekin dishes, and sprinkle them with parsley (or dill) and half of the grated cheese.

Make a béchamel sauce with 30 g (2 tbsp) of butter, the flour and the milk. Add the wine and season with salt, pepper and lemon juice. Pour 3 tbsp of sauce on top of each ramekin. Sprinkle with the remaining grated cheese, breadcrumbs, and cayenne pepper; dot sparingly with the remaining butter. Bake in an oven preheated to 200°C (400°F) for 15 minutes, or until hot and lightly browned.

Serves 6 as a first course

Meat Bourekákia

Μπουρεκάκια με Κρέας

The half-moon shape is traditional for bourekákia, as is the triangle or short cylinder. These small pastries may be filled with many of the same fillings used for pítas, such as cheese, spinach, chicken, etc. They are particularly attractive when both shapes and fillings are varied. Count on two to three bourekákia per person when serving a variety of mezés.

Pastry
225 g (1½ cups) flour
1½ tsp baking powder
1 tsp salt
8 cl (⅓ cup) milk
8 cl (⅓ cup) olive oil
2 tbsp water to mix
Filling
500 gr (1 lb) ground beef
1 medium-sized onion, finely chopped
1 tbsp olive oil
1 medium-sized tomato, peeled, seeded and chopped
2 tbsp finely chopped parsley
1 hot red pepper, seeded, or ¼ tsp dried red pepper
Salt and freshly ground black pepper
Oil for deep frying

Combine all the pastry ingredients, adding enough water to make a thick dough. Refrigerate for at least one hour.

To prepare the filling, sauté the onion in the oil, add the meat, tomato, parsley and red pepper, and season with salt and pepper. Simmer 20 to 25 minutes, until all the liquid is absorbed. Remove the red pepper if used whole.

Roll out the pastry to 3 mm (⅛ in) thick, and cut it into circles 8 cm (3 in) in diameter. Place a heaping teaspoon of filling on one half of each circle, fold over and pinch the sides to stick together.

Deep-fry in hot oil until golden brown. Drain on paper towels and serve them warm.

Makes 40 bourekákia

Cheese Bourekákia

Μπουρεκάκια με Τυρί

You may freeze the uncooked bourekákia in the muffin tins for several days.
Defrost them for three hours before baking as directed.

Pastry
300 g (2 cups) flour
2 tsp baking powder
½ tsp salt
125 g (4 oz or ½ cup) butter
8 cl (⅓ cup) milk
Filling
250 g (2 cups) féta cheese, crumbled
250 g (2 cups) grated cheese, a combination of kaséri,
Gruyère, Gouda or Edam
1 tbsp flour
1 tbsp milk
¼ tsp sugar
Nutmeg
Pepper
3 eggs, well beaten
1 egg, slightly beaten
1 tbsp grated kephalotýri or Parmesan cheese
Paprika

To make the pastry, sift together the flour, baking powder and salt. Cut
in the butter, add the milk and knead until smooth.
Combine all the filling ingredients, except the eggs. Slowly beat in the
3 eggs to make a thick mixture.
Roll out the pastry to 3 mm (⅛ in), and cut it into 8 cm (3 in) rounds.
Line the muffin tins with the pastry. Divide the filling among the muffin
tins. Brush with the remaining egg, and sprinkle with the grated cheese
and paprika.
Bake in an oven preheated to 180°C (350°F) for 15 to 20 minutes, until
golden brown.
Makes 45 bourekákia

Cheese Puffs

Τυροκεφτέδες

This recipe makes good use of leftover egg whites.

125 g (1 cup) grated kephalotýri or Parmesan cheese
2 tbsp flour
3 egg whites, beaten stiff
60 g (½ cup) flour
Parsley sprigs

Fold the cheese and 2 tbsp flour into the egg whites to make a thick
paste. Shape the mixture into walnut-size balls. Roll them in flour and
deep-fry in oil until golden.
Drain on paper towels. Serve the cheese puffs with a sprig of parsley
held in place with a toothpick.
Makes 15 puffs

Ham and Cheese Puffs

Σβιγκάκια με Ζαμπόν και Τυρί

Filling
125 g (1 cup) grated kephalotýri or Parmesan cheese
3 to 4 slices of ham, chopped
2 tbsp butter at room temperature
Chou pastry
35 cl (1½ cups) water
1 tsp salt
2 tbsp butter
225 g (1½ cups) flour
3 eggs

Combine the filling ingredients and set aside.
To prepare the chou pastry, bring the water, salt and butter to the boil.
Remove from the heat and stir in the flour. When thoroughly combined,
cook and stir over medium heat until the mixture cleans the sides of the
saucepan. Cool for several minutes.
Transfer the dough to a food processor, add the eggs and process until
smooth. If you have no food processor, you may add the eggs to the
pan, one at a time, beating well after each addition.
Shape the mixture into walnut-size balls and bake on a buttered baking
tin in an oven preheated to 190° C (375° F) for 15 to 20 minutes, or until
the pastry is puffed and golden brown. Remove from the oven and turn
off the heat.
Puncture each puff with a knife, letting the hot air escape. Return the
pastry to the oven for 10 minutes without additional heat. Remove them,
and cool on a rack.
When cool, cut each puff in half and stuff with the filling. Press together
and serve.
Makes 35 to 40 puffs

Cheese Saganáki

Σαγανάκι

*Saganáki is the name of the small two-handled frying pan in which this cheese
dish is traditionally cooked and served. Success lies in serving the saganáki
just at the moment the cheese begins to melt.*

1 slice of Kephalotýri or Gruyère cheese, 1 cm (½ in) thick
1 tbsp butter
2 tbsp flour
¼ lemon

Melt the butter in a small frying pan. Dredge the cheese in the flour and
sauté on both sides in the butter until golden brown. Squeeze the lemon
over the saganáki and serve in the pan.
Variation: Fry an egg, a sausage, or a slice of bacon, ham, or salami in
the pan next to the cheese. And try different types of cheese, such as
raclette, blue cheese or féta.
Serves 1

Soups

Avgolémono Soup

Σούπα Αυγολέμονο

To achieve and maintain a delicately smooth consistency, never cover the soup pot when preparing or heating this soup.

3 liters (12 cups) chicken, meat or fish stock (or stock made from meat or chicken bouillon cubes)
75 g (6 tbsp) short grain rice or small pasta
2 eggs at room temperature, separated
2 lemons, juice only
Salt and freshly ground black pepper

In a heavy saucepan, boil the stock, add the rice and cook until soft, about 20 minutes. Remove the saucepan from the heat. Beat the egg whites until fairly stiff.
In another bowl, beat the yolks until creamy, then beat the lemon juice into them. Gently fold the yolks into the egg whites.
Very slowly, add about ½ liter (2 cups) of the stock to the eggs, stirring quickly. Pour this mixture slowly back into the remaining stock, stirring constantly. With the pot uncovered, gently reheat the soup, still stirring. Season with salt and pepper and serve.
Serves 6 to 8

June's Spinach Soup

Σπανακόσουπα

Although not a traditionally Greek use for spinach, this recipe is inspired by the incredible quality, freshness and flavor of the local spinach, available during the cooler half of the year.

1 kg (2 lb) fresh spinach, chopped
2 green onions, chopped
2 garlic cloves, finely chopped
30 g (2 tbsp) butter
1 tbsp flour
Pinch of nutmeg
½ liter (2 cups) chicken stock
2 tbsp finely chopped dill
Salt and freshly ground black pepper
¼ liter (1 cup) cream

In a large saucepan, sauté the onions and garlic in butter until soft. Add the flour and nutmeg, cook and stir for two to three minutes. Mix in the spinach and stirring constantly, add the stock. Simmer for 10 minutes; add the dill. Process or purée the soup.
Return the soup to the saucepan. Season it with salt and pepper, stir in all but 1 tbsp of the cream and reheat slowly. Serve the soup with the remaining cream floating on top.
Serves 6 to 8

Magerítsa

Μαγειρίτσα

During the forty days of Lent, the more traditional of the Greek Orthodox refrain from eating meat, eggs, milk and butter. Easter is celebrated with a long church service which ends at midnight on Saturday. The priest comes out of church carrying a candle, the light of which symbolizes the resurrection of Christ. The light from the priest's candle is passed around the congregation, as each person from the very oldest to the very youngest holds his own candle. Church bells chime, teenagers shoot off fireworks and everyone exclaims "Christós Anésti", which means "Christ is risen". Kisses are exchanged among family and friends, and by one in the morning, most participants have settled down to the business of eating magerítsa and breaking their fast. Easter is the highlight of the church year in Greece, and is exciting to experience regardless of one's religion. Magerítsa, although delicious on its own, benefits from its association with this annual midnight celebration.

1 kg (2 lb) lamb liver, kidneys, spleen and heart (or substitute leg
of lamb, stewing beef and/or chicken parts, cut in small pieces)
1 tbsp flour diluted in 12 cl (½ cup) cold water
4 to 5 green onions, chopped
4 tbsp finely chopped dill
4 tbsp finely chopped parsley
30 g (2 tbsp) butter
75 g (6 tbsp) short grain rice, or 1 tbsp per person
3 eggs at room temperature, separated
2 lemons, juice only
Salt and freshly ground black pepper

Wash the lamb parts (or meat) very well. Reserving the liver, place the rest in a saucepan of cold water and bring to the boil. Strain and discard the water. Place the lamb parts in a saucepan of fresh hot water, stir in the flour diluted in water, and some salt. Simmer for 30 minutes, or until tender. Strain and reserve the liquid; chop the lamb parts into very small pieces.

If using liver, chop it in small pieces. Sauté it together with the green onions, dill and parsley in the butter until soft, about five minutes. Add the lamb parts and liver-herb mixture to the reserved liquid and bring to the boil. Add the rice and simmer until tender, about 20 minutes. Remove from heat.

In a bowl, beat the egg whites until fairly stiff. Beat the yolks and lemon juice very well and add them gently to the egg whites.

Gradually add ½ liter (2 cups) of the soup to the egg mixture, stirring constantly. Still stirring, gradually add the egg mixture to the soup. Season with salt and pepper and reheat slowly without boiling, stirring constantly. The magerítsa should be served fairly warm, but not hot.

Serves 6 to 8

Fasoláda
Φασολάδα

This bean soup, with more or less vegetable seasoning according to family and local tastes, is known as "the soup that nourishes Greece" and "the meat of the poor". It is available everywhere in winter months, even in the most remote of mountain villages, and is hearty, nourishing and memorable. One can't reduce the amount of olive oil without the end result suffering!

500 g (1 lb) dried white haricot or cannellini beans, soaked
overnight in 2 liters (8 cups) water, and drained
2 potatoes, peeled and cubed
1 medium-sized onion, chopped
2 carrots, sliced
6 celery sticks, chopped
2 tbsp finely chopped parsley
2 liters (8 cups) water
25 cl (1 cup) olive oil
380 g (12 oz) tinned tomatoes, puréed, or 2 tbsp tomato paste diluted
in 12 cl (½ cup) water
Salt and freshly ground black pepper
Lemon wedges

If the beans you are using are less than one year old, they shouldn't really need soaking. In a large saucepan, cover the beans with cold water, bring them to the boil, and simmer for five minutes. Strain and discard the water in which they have been boiled.

Put the beans, potatoes, onion, carrots, celery and parsley in a large saucepan and cover with the 2 liters (8 cups) of unsalted water. Bring to the boil and simmer, partly covered, for one hour, or until the beans are tender. If necessary, add boiling water to prevent sticking. Stir in the olive oil and puréed tomatoes (or diluted tomato paste) and boil vigorously for 10 minutes more, or until the soup thickens. Season with salt and pepper and serve with lemon wedges.

Variation: Sauté ¼ tsp of cayenne pepper in the olive oil before adding it to the soup, as they do in northern Greece where the weather is cold.

You may sieve or process the soup before serving it with croutons.

Serves 6 to 8

Chick Pea Soup

Ρεβιθόσουπα

Revíthia, as it is known in Greek, is a soup which has as many secrets as cooks who prepare it. The challenge presented by the chick peas is to get them to soften. To achieve this goal, some recommend using only wooden spoons, or never salting the soup before the peas soften, or using several changes of rainwater to soak the chick peas, or using baking soda, or not using baking soda, etc. All secrets considered, always soak the chick peas overnight and have patience in cooking them because it does take a long time. But the most important element in success is having good quality and relatively fresh chick peas. If after two hours your peas show no sign of softening, you may assume defeat by a poor quality of chick pea. But do try again. Chick pea soup is simple, robust and tasty. The soup itself is made up of the chick peas, which in general remain whole, and the broth which thickens while cooking with the olive oil. Strained leftover chick peas are a delicious addition to a green or mixed salad.

500 g (1 lb) dried chick peas, skinned if available
1 tbsp baking soda (if chick peas are not skinned)
1½ liters (6 cups) water
25 cl (1 cup) olive oil
1 large onion, finely chopped
2 carrots, cubed
4 tbsp finely chopped parsley
Salt and freshly ground black pepper
Lemon wedges

Place the chick peas in an earthenware or glass bowl, cover with luke-warm water and soak overnight.

If the chick peas are not skinned, treat them as follows: after soaking, drain the chick peas in a colander, sprinkle with the baking soda and stir. Let them stand for 15 minutes, then wash with hot water and drain. Taking several at a time, rub them with a towel to remove skins. Wash thoroughly.

In a large saucepan cover the chick peas with the water and bring to the boil. Skim off the foam as it forms. Add the olive oil, onion, carrots and parsley; simmer slowly with the saucepan half-covered for one hour, or until the chick peas are soft. Season with salt and pepper and serve with lemon wedges.

Serves 6 to 8

Lentil Soup

Φακές

Lentil soup is a nation-wide favorite, and is generally prepared at home rather than as taverna fare. Lentils cook up quickly into an inexpensive and filling meal. Use either large or small lentils, and as many of the aromatic vegetables as you like.

500g (1lb) brown lentils
2 medium-sized onions, finely chopped
2 medium-sized potatoes, cubed
2 carrots, cubed
3 celery sticks, finely chopped
2 tbsp finely chopped parsley
3 garlic cloves, finely chopped
2 bay leaves
2 liters (8 cups) water
25 cl (1 cup) olive oil
380 g (12 oz) tinned tomatoes, puréed, or 2 tbsp tomato paste diluted in 12 cl (½ cup) water
Salt and freshly ground black pepper
2 tsp oregano

In a large saucepan, cover the lentils, onions, potatoes, carrots, celery, parsley, garlic and bay leaves with cold unsalted water. Boil for 30 minutes, or until all the vegetables are tender.

Add the olive oil, puréed tomatoes (or diluted tomato paste), and salt and pepper to taste. Boil vigorously for five minutes more, stirring occasionally. The soup should be fairly thick. Stir in the oregano.

Serve with olive oil and vinegar, to be added to individual taste at the table.

Serves 6 to 8

Split Pea Soup

Μπιζελόσουπα

500 g (1 lb) green split peas
2 liters (8 cups) meat stock or water
1 large onion, finely chopped
2 carrots, sliced
3 celery sticks, finely chopped
30 g (2 tbsp) butter
Salt and freshly ground black pepper
1 tbsp finely chopped parsley

In a large saucepan, cover the peas with the water or stock. Bring to the boil and skim well as foam forms. Meanwhile, sauté the onion, carrots and celery in the butter until soft. Add these to the peas and simmer until peas are soft, about one hour.

The soup may be thinned to desired consistency with hot water, if necessary. Season with salt and pepper and sprinkle with parsley.

Serves 6 to 8

Potato Soup Marinos

Πατατόσουπα

Just the right soup for a bitter cold day.

6 medium-sized potatoes, sliced 1 cm (½ in) thick
1 large carrot, sliced
4 garlic cloves, crushed with 1 tsp salt
1 tbsp butter
1½ liters (6 cups) chicken stock
½ liter (2 cups) milk
Salt and freshly ground black pepper
Cayenne pepper
Nutmeg
8 cl (⅓ cup) cream
2 tbsp finely chopped parsley

Melt the butter in a large saucepan and in it sauté the potatoes, carrots
and garlic for 15 minutes, stirring occasionally. Add the chicken stock
and simmer until the vegetables are tender, about 30 minutes. You may
then either pass the vegetables through a sieve, or purée them until
smooth in a food processor.
Return the soup to the saucepan, stir in the milk and reheat it slowly,
without boiling. Season with salt, pepper, cayenne pepper and nutmeg
to taste. Serve in individual bowls, topped with a spoonful of cream and
sprinkled with parsley.
Serves 6

Vegetable Soup

Χορτόσουπα

*Although the diet of Greeks includes a substantial and healthy quantity of
vegetables, this soup has foreign inspiration.*

2 medium-sized potatoes, cubed
3 carrots, cubed
25 g (½ cup) chopped parsley
3 celery sticks, chopped
2 medium-sized onions, chopped
1 or 2 turnips, sliced
1 leek, sliced
1½ liters (6 cups) water
12 cl (½ cup) tomato juice
Salt and freshly ground black pepper
1 tbsp butter

Cover the vegetables with the water and simmer for 30 minutes, until
soft. Add the tomato juice and season with salt and pepper. You may
either purée the soup or serve it as it is. Stir in butter before serving.
Serves 6 to 8

Pasta
& Grains

Tomato Sauce

Σάλτσα Ντομάτας

6 fresh tomatoes, halved, seeded and grated, skins discarded
50 g (3 tbsp) butter
½ tsp sugar
Salt and freshly ground black pepper
1 bay leaf
2 sprigs fresh basil or mint
2 garlic cloves crushed with 1 tsp salt (optional)

Simmer all ingredients slowly for 30 to 35 minutes, or until the sauce thickens. Remove the bay leaf and sprigs of mint or basil. Serve over spaghetti or with croquettes.
Serves 4 to 6

Summer Pasta

Καλοκαιρινή Μακαρονάδα

500 g (1 lb) penne or other thick cut pasta
3 fresh tomatoes, cut in eighths
250 g (2 cups) grated kephalotýri or Parmesan cheese
90 g (6 tbsp) butter, at room temperature
2 or 3 garlic cloves, crushed
6 tbsp chopped fresh basil
Freshly ground black pepper

In a serving bowl, combine the cheese, butter, garlic and basil. Boil the penne in plenty of salted water until *al dente*. Drain, transfer to the serving bowl and mix well. Add the tomatoes, plenty of black pepper, mix again and serve immediately.
Serves 4 to 6

Tomato Sauce with Celery

Σάλτσα Ντομάτας με Σέλινο

6 medium-sized tomatoes, halved, seeded and grated,
skins discarded
1 medium-sized onion, grated
50 g (3 tbsp) butter or olive oil
6 celery sticks with leaves, finely chopped
¼ liter (1 cup) dry white wine
3 tbsp finely chopped parsley
1 bay leaf
Salt and freshly ground black pepper
½ tsp sugar
60 g (½ cup) grated kephalotýri or Parmesan cheese

Sauté the onion in the butter or olive oil until it is transparent. Add the remaining ingredients, except the pasta and grated cheese. Simmer for 30 minutes, or until the sauce thickens.
Boil the sedani in plenty of salted water until just tender; drain and transfer to a warmed bowl. After removing the bay leaf from the sauce, serve it over sedani (celery-shaped pasta), sprinkled with grated cheese.
Serves 5 to 6

Devilled Spaghettini

Πικάντικη Σπαγγετίνι

*This unusually flavored pasta dish doesn't require grated cheese; the cream
makes the difference.*

500 g (1 lb) spaghettini
6 medium-sized tomatoes, halved, seeded and grated,
skins discarded
4 garlic cloves, crushed
1 tbsp olive oil
1 sprig of rosemary
1 tbsp Mavrodáphne (or other sweet red wine)
50 g (3 tbsp) butter
½ tsp cayenne pepper
Salt
¼ liter (1 cup) cream

Simmer the tomatoes, garlic, olive oil, wine, rosemary and 1 tbsp butter
together for 20 minutes. Season with the cayenne pepper and salt.
Remove from the heat and add the cream, stirring well. Set aside.
Boil the spaghettini in plenty of salted water until *al dente*. Drain and mix
well with the remaining butter and sauce. Serve immediately in a
warmed bowl.
Serves 4 to 6

Penne with Ragoût Sauce

Μακαρόνια με Σάλτσα Ραγκού

This seasoned tomato sauce is vegetarian and excellent to serve during Lent.

500 g (1 lb) penne or other thick cut pasta
4 medium-sized onions, sliced
6 medium-sized tomatoes, halved, seeded and grated,
skins discarded
4 tbsp olive oil
4 or 5 cinnamon sticks
½ tsp sugar
Salt and freshly ground black pepper

Sauté the onions in the olive oil until soft. Add the remaining ingredients
and simmer slowly, partly covered, for 30 minutes, or until the sauce
thickens.
Cook the penne in plenty of boiling salted water, drain and transfer to a
warmed bowl. After removing the cinnamon sticks from the sauce,
serve it hot over the penne.
Serves 4 to 5

Pastítsio

Παστίτσιο

Pastítsio is a great dish to feed a large and hungry family. A Zantiote friend told me that he celebrated the end of World War II with an enormous pastítsio of his own concoction. Its many, many layers included chicken, meatballs, hard-boiled eggs, meat, hare stew, and of course macaroni! This dish freezes well, and individual servings can be frozen until needed, then defrosted and heated in a microwave or oven. Pastítsio is particularly a children's favorite.

500 g (1 lb) bucatini or ziti (long hollow macaroni)
90 g (6 tbsp) butter or margerine
1 egg, beaten
1 medium-sized onion, finely chopped
1 kg (2 lbs) ground beef
¼ lit (1 cup) red or white wine
3 medium-sized tomatoes, halved, seeded, and grated,
skins discarded
25 g (½ cup) finely chopped parsley
1 tsp oregano
Salt and freshly ground black pepper
½ tsp sugar
60 g (½ cup) grated kephalotýri or Parmesan cheese
2 tbsp breadcrumbs
2 tbsp butter
Béchamel Sauce
120 g (4 oz) butter
75 g (½ cup) flour
1 liter (1 qt) hot milk
60 g (½ cup) grated kephalotýri or Parmesan cheese
2 eggs, lightly beaten
Pinch of nutmeg
Salt and freshly ground black pepper

Boil the macaroni in plenty of salted water until *al dente*. Drain in a colander, then rinse lightly with cold water. Return the macaroni to its pot and stir in half the butter and the beaten egg. Set aside.

Melt the rest of the butter in a large skillet and sauté the onion until transparent. Add the ground beef and sauté 10 minutes more, stirring well to break up the meat. Add the wine, tomatoes, parsley and oregano. Season with salt, pepper and sugar. Simmer uncovered until all the liquid has evaporated, about 20 minutes.

Meanwhile, prepare the béchamel sauce. Melt the butter in a large saucepan; add the flour and cook for 3 to 4 minutes, stirring constantly. Add the hot milk gradually, gently stirring all the time as the sauce comes to the boil and thickens. Remove from heat and stir in most of the cheese. Let cool slightly, then stir in the eggs and season to taste with salt, pepper and nutmeg.

Spread several spoonfuls of the meat mixture over the bottom of a 30 by 45 cm (12 by 18 in) baking dish. Make a layer of half of the macaroni, then evenly spread the meat sauce over. Cover with the rest of the macaroni. Pour the béchamel sauce over all. Sprinkle with the remaining grated cheese and the breadcrumbs, and dot with 2 tbsp butter.

Bake in a moderate oven preheated to 190°C (375°F), for about one hour, until golden brown. Let cool slightly before cutting into squares.
Serves 12

Pastitsáda

Παστιτσάδα

This is a traditional dish from the island of Corfu.

1 kg (2 lb) lean beef or veal, cut in 3 cm (1 inch) cubes
500 g (1 lb) bucatini (long hollow macaroni)
3 medium-sized onions, finely chopped
12 cl (½ cup) olive oil
2 tbsp tomato paste
12 cl (½ cup) white wine
1 tbsp vinegar
2 whole cloves
1 stick cinnamon
1 tsp cayenne pepper (or less if preferred)
½ tsp black pepper
50 g (3 tbsp) butter, melted
60 g (½ cup) grated kephalotýri or Parmesan cheese

Sauté the meat and onions in the olive oil until slightly browned. Add the tomato paste, wine, vinegar, cloves, cinnamon, cayenne and black pepper. Simmer for 1½ hours, or until the meat is tender. Add hot water if necessary to prevent sticking.
Boil the macaroni in plenty of salted water until *al dente;* drain and transfer it to a warmed bowl. Pour the melted butter over the macaroni and sprinkle with the grated cheese. Serve the meat over the macaroni or in a separate bowl.
Serves 8 to 10

Tomato Sauce with Chopped Meat

Ντομάτα Σάλτσα με Κιμά

500 g (1 lb) chopped beef or veal
3 tbsp butter or olive oil
1 medium-sized onion, finely chopped
3 tbsp finely chopped parsley
12 cl (½ cup) red wine
4 medium-sized tomatoes, halved, seeded and grated,
skins discarded
1 clove garlic, finely chopped
2 bay leaves
Salt and freshly ground black pepper
½ tsp sugar

Heat the oil or butter in a frying pan, then add the onion and sauté until soft. Add the chopped meat and sauté until all the liquid evaporates. Stir in the wine and the remaining ingredients, and simmer for about 30 minutes. Remove the bay leaves and serve over spaghetti or noodles.
Serves 4 to 6

Tagliatelle with Three Cheeses

Χυλοπίτες με Τρία Τυριά

A Greek version of macaroni and cheese, which is, like our own favorite, filling, fattening and delicious.

500 g (1 lb) tagliatelle or tagliatelle verdi
60 g (4 tbsp) butter
125 g (1 cup) féta cheese, cubed
125 g (1 cup) Gruyère cheese, cubed
125 g (1 cup) kaséri cheese, cubed
Freshly ground black pepper
½ liter (2 cups) cream

Boil the tagliatelle in plenty of salted water until *al dente;* drain. Mix immediately with the butter, cheeses and plenty of pepper. Transfer to a large buttered baking dish, pour the cream over and bake in an oven preheated to 190°C (375°F) for 30 minutes, or until golden brown. *Variation:* Add 250 g (8 oz) of chopped ham, fried bacon or sautéed mushrooms to the tagliatelle when mixing in the cheeses.

Serves 8 to 10

Clams and Linguine

Αχηβάδες Σπαγγετίνι

500 g (1 lb) fresh clams or oysters, or one 200 g (7 oz) tin
500 g (1 lb) linguine or spaghettini
3 small hot red peppers, whole
2 garlic cloves, whole
8 cl (⅓ cup) olive oil
2 tbsp finely chopped parsley
3 medium-sized tomatoes, halved, seeded and grated, skins discarded
1 medium-sized onion, whole
1 bay leaf
½ tsp sugar
Salt and freshly ground black pepper

Sauté the red peppers and garlic in half the olive oil. Add the clams (or oysters) and parsley, stir well and remove from the heat. Discard the peppers and garlic.

Simmer the remaining olive oil, the tomatoes, onion, bay leaf, sugar, salt and pepper together in another saucepan for 30 minutes. Remove and discard the onion and bay leaf. Meanwhile, boil the linguine in plenty of salted water until *al dente;* drain.

Process or sieve the tomato mixture and add it to the clams. Heat and serve over the freshly boiled linguine or spaghettini.

Serves 4 to 6

Orzo Pilaf with Tomatoes

Κριθαράκι με Ντομάτα Πιλάφι

Simple and inexpensive, this is very popular with children.

500 g (1 lb) orzo
3 medium-sized tomatoes, halved, seeded and grated,
skins discarded
1 medium-sized onion, grated
60 g (4 tbsp) butter or olive oil
1 liter (4 cups) water
1 bay leaf
Salt and freshly ground black pepper
½ tsp sugar
125 g (1 cup) grated kephalotýri or Parmesan cheese

In a medium-sized saucepan, sauté the onion in the butter (or olive oil) until transparent. Add the tomatoes, water, bay leaf, salt, pepper and sugar, and simmer for five minutes. Add the orzo and stir until it boils. Simmer, covered, over low heat for 15 to 20 minutes, or until the orzo is cooked and liquid has been absorbed. If necessary, add more boiling water to prevent sticking. Serve sprinkled with the grated cheese.
Variation: Prepare the orzo without tomatoes, substituting 1 liter (4 cups) of chicken or beef stock for the water. Or try substituting couscous or peponaki (small melon seed-shaped pasta) for the orzo.
Serves 4 to 6

Orzo with Lentils

Φακές «Φακομάτσο»

250 g (½ lb) lentils
200 g (1 cup) orzo
2 large onions, finely chopped
12 cl (½ cup) olive oil
2 medium-sized tomatoes, halved, seeded and grated,
skins discarded
Salt and freshly ground black pepper
¼ tsp sugar

In a large saucepan, cover the lentils with cold water, bring to the boil and simmer for 5 minutes. Drain and set aside. Sauté the onions in the olive oil until transparent.

Combine the lentils, onions, oil and tomatoes in a flameproof casserole. Cover with cold water, bring to the boil and simmer for 45 minutes, or until the lentils are just tender. Add the orzo and simmer another 20 minutes. If necessary, add a little hot water to prevent sticking. Season with salt, pepper and the sugar, and serve.

Serves 6

Plain Pilaf

Πιλάφι Σκέτο

This recipe uses unprocessed long grain rice. If you use parboiled rice, prepare it according to package directions.

400 g (2 cups) long grain rice
2 liters (8 cups) water
1½ tsp salt
2 tbsp butter, melted

Boil the rice in the salted water for 20 minutes, or until just done. Drain, rinse with cold water and drain again. Return the rice to the saucepan, reheat it and pour the butter over.

Accompaniments for Plain Pilaf

Baked Tomatoes: Remove the core from whole red ripe tomatoes, top them with a knob of butter and sprinkle with salt, pepper and sugar. Bake in an oven preheated to 190°C (375°F) for 35 to 40 minutes. Serve with the pilaf and pass plenty of grated cheese.

Sautéed Chicken Livers: Sauté 250 g (8 oz) of chopped chicken livers in butter. Season with salt, pepper and oregano and serve over pilaf.

Avgolémono: Make ½ liter (2 cups) of avgolémono sauce, page 95, using chicken or beef stock, and serve over the pilaf.

Chicken Béchamel: To ½ liter (2 cups) of thin béchamel sauce, add 300 g (2 cups) of skinless cooked chicken. Flavor it with plenty of lemon juice and chopped parsley, and serve over the pilaf.

Fish Béchamel: To ½ liter (2 cups) of béchamel sauce, add 300 g (2 cups) of cooked white fish. Flavor it with a bay leaf, plenty of lemon juice and chopped parsley, and serve over pilaf.

Spanikó: Sauté 150 g (1 cup) of peas and 125 g (4 oz) of chopped ham in 2 tbsp butter and stir into pilaf. Serve with tomato sauce, page 40, and top with grated cheese.

Serves 6 to 8

Shrimp Pilaf

Πιλάφι με Γαρίδες

750 g (1½ lb) shrimp, washed and black intestines removed
400 g (2 cups) long grain rice
2 medium-sized onions, one whole and one chopped
1 celery stick
1 bay leaf
1½ liters (6 cups) water
1 tbsp salt
6 cl (¼ cup) olive oil
4 large tomatoes, seeded and grated, skins discarded
Salt and freshly ground black pepper
Cayenne pepper
½ tsp sugar
30 g (2 tbsp) fresh butter
5 or 6 parsley sprigs

Boil the whole onion, celery and bay leaf in the water for 20 minutes. Add the shrimp and 1 tbsp salt. Boil for five minutes, then set aside to cool in the cooking liquid. When cool, drain the shrimp and reserve the cooking liquid. Peel them and set aside.

Heat the olive oil in a saucepan and sauté the chopped onion until transparent. Add the tomatoes and season with salt, pepper, cayenne pepper and sugar. Simmer for 20 minutes. In a heavy saucepan, boil 4 cups of shrimp liquid and the butter. Add the rice, stir well, then cover the saucepan tightly with a cloth and lid, and simmer very, very slowly until all the liquid is absorbed, about 30 minutes.

To serve, reheat the tomato sauce and stir in most of the shrimp. Transfer the rice to a serving dish and decorate it with the remaining shrimp and sprigs of parsley. Serve the sauce in a separate bowl.

Serves 6

Green Pepper Pilaf

Πιλάφι με Πιπεριές

400 g (2 cups) long grain rice
3 large green peppers, thinly sliced
1 medium-sized onion, thinly sliced
4 tbsp olive oil
2 celery sticks, finely chopped
2 tbsp finely chopped parsley
6 medium tomatoes, seeded and grated, skins discarded
1 liter (4 cups) boiling water
Salt and freshly ground black pepper
½ tsp sugar
1 tbsp chopped fresh basil

Stirring occasionally, sauté the green peppers and onion in the olive oil for 10 minutes, until soft. Add the tomatoes, celery, and parsley, and simmer slowly, uncovered, until the liquid has evaporated.

Add the rice and boiling water; season with salt, pepper, sugar and basil. Return to the boil, reduce heat, cover with a cloth and lid, and simmer very, very slowly for 30 minutes, or until all the liquid has been absorbed. Do not stir. Serve the pilaf either hot or at room temperature.

Serves 8

Spanakóryzo

Σπανακόρυζο

Frozen spinach is no substitute for fresh spinach in this recipe. Remove all yellow or brown leaves and the very bottoms of the stems. Wash the spinach well before chopping it.

200 g (1 cup) long grain rice
1 kg (2 lb) spinach, coarsely chopped
1 medium-sized onion, finely chopped
4 green onions, finely chopped
12 cl (½ cup) olive oil
3 tbsp finely chopped dill
3 medium-sized tomatoes, halved, seeded and grated,
skins discarded
Salt and freshly ground black pepper
¼ tsp sugar
¼ liter (1 cup) boiling water

In a large saucepan, sauté the onions and scallions in the oil for five minutes, until soft. Add the spinach and dill, and simmer until these are soft, stirring occasionally. Add the tomatoes, season with salt, pepper and sugar, and simmer another five minutes. Add the rice and water, cover with a cloth and lid, and simmer very, very slowly for 30 to 40 minutes, or until all the liquid has been absorbed.

Variation: Omit the tomatoes, increase the water to ½ liter (2 cups) and serve with lemon wedges. Swiss chard also makes an interesting substitute for spinach.

Serves 4 to 6

Leeks and Rice

Πρασόρυζο

One effective way to ensure that the leeks contain no sand is to parboil them for a few minutes before rinsing them and proceeding with the recipe. Served with olives and fresh bread, leeks and rice make an excellent vegetarian meal.

400 g (2 cups) long grain rice
1 kg (2 lb) leeks, trimmed, finely sliced and washed
8 celery sticks, chopped
4 tbsp (¼ cup) olive oil
Salt and freshly ground black pepper
1 liter (4 cups) boiling beef or chicken stock
Lemon wedges

In a large saucepan, sauté the leeks and celery in the olive oil for about 20 minutes, until soft and liquid has evaporated. Season with salt and pepper, add the rice and stir well. Add boiling stock, cover the saucepan with a cloth and lid, and simmer very, very slowly for about 30 minutes, or until all the liquid has been absorbed. Garnish with lemon wedges.

Serves 6 to 8

Eggplant Pilaf

Μελιτζάνες Πιλάφι

When eggplant are expensive, this is a most economical and delicious way to serve them.

200 g (1 cup) long grain rice
500 g (1 lb) long slim eggplant, unpeeled and cut crosswise into very thin slices
3 small onions, very thinly sliced
4 tbsp olive oil or butter
4 large tomatoes, halved, seeded and grated, skins discarded
25 g (½ cup) finely chopped parsley
Salt and freshly ground black pepper
½ tsp sugar
½ liter (2 cups) boiling water
1 green pepper, thinly sliced
Chopped parsley

In a heavy saucepan, sauté the eggplant and onion in the olive oil for 20 minutes, stirring occasionally, until the mixture just begins to stick to the pan. Be careful not to let the onions brown too much. Add tomatoes, parsley, salt, pepper and sugar to taste; simmer until the liquid evaporates. Add the rice, cook and stir for a few minutes. Add the boiling water. Cover the saucepan with a cloth and lid and simmer very, very slowly for about 30 minutes, or until all the liquid is absorbed. To serve, press the rice into an oiled mold, leave for 3 or 4 minutes, then turn out on a serving dish and garnish with thin slices of green pepper and chopped parsley.

Serves 4 to 6

Christmas Pilaf

Χριστουγεννιάτικο Πιλάφι

Christmas takes a second place to New Year's when it comes to celebrating in Greece. A traditional Christmas dinner might include this dish.

500 g (2½ cups) long grain rice
1 kg (2 lb) chestnuts, boiled for 5 minutes and shelled
1 medium-sized onion, finely chopped
60 g (4 tbsp) butter
2 tbsp pine nuts
75 g (½ cup) dried apricots, chopped
100 g (½ cup) prunes, stoned and chopped
75 g (½ cup) seedless raisins or sultánas
6 celery sticks, finely chopped
25 g (½ cup) finely chopped parsley
Salt and freshly ground black pepper
1.75 liters (7 cups) boiling stock or 2 buillon cubes dissolved
in 1.75 liters (7 cups) hot water
3 tbsp red vermouth

In a saucepan sauté the onion in 50 g (3 tbsp) of butter until transparent. Add half of the chestnuts and the pine nuts and sauté until slightly brown. Stir in the rice, apricots, prunes, raisins, celery and parsley. Season with salt and black pepper. Add 1.25 liters (5 cups) of the boiling stock, return to the boil, and cover with a cloth and lid. Simmer very, very slowly for 30 minutes, or until all the liquid has been absorbed. Meanwhile, place the remaining chestnuts in a small ovenproof dish. Cover with the remaining stock, the vermouth and the rest of the butter. Sprinkle with salt and pepper and braise in the bottom of an oven pre-heated to 190°C (375°F) for 45 minutes, or until the chestnuts are soft. To serve, transfer the pilaf to a serving dish and garnish with the braised chestnuts. This pilaf is an excellent first course or a buffet dish to accompany roast turkey or chicken.

Serves 10 to 12

Pies

Tyrópita

Τυρόπιτα

Tyrópita in its many forms is the basic snack of Greece, eaten any time from early morning breakfast to late night supper. It's as easy to make as it is to eat. This is a good basic recipe from which to start Greek pie making.

Filling
500 g (1 lb) féta cheese, grated or crumbled
3 tbsp grated kephalotýri or Parmesan cheese
30 g (2 tbsp) butter
2 tbsp flour
½ liter (2 cups) milk
4 eggs, lightly beaten
4 tbsp finely chopped parsley
¼ tsp nutmeg
½ tsp sugar
Salt and freshly ground black pepper
Pastry
500 g (1 lb) phýllo pastry
175 g (6 oz) melted butter or margarine

First prepare the filling. Make a béchamel sauce with the butter, flour and milk, (see page 42), and leave it to cool slightly. Combine the cheeses in a large bowl. Add the sauce to the cheese and stir in the eggs. Add the parsley and season with nutmeg, sugar, salt and pepper. Line a rectangular baking tin, 30 by 45 cm (12 by 18 in), or a 35 cm (14 in) round baking tin with 5 or 6 sheets of phýllo, brushing each sheet liberally with the melted butter. Allow the excess pastry to overhang the pan. Spread the cheese mixture over the phýllo and place another 5 or 6 sheets of pastry on top, again brushing each sheet with melted butter. Trim off all but 5 cm (2 in) of the overhanging phýllo with a pair of kitchen scissors. Fold over the phýllo to form an edging around the pie. Brush the edging with melted butter and with a knife, score the top layers of phýllo into squares. Sprinkle the tyrópita with a little cold water and bake in a moderate oven preheated to 190°C (375°F) for one hour.

To serve, cool the tyrópita for 15 minutes, then cut it into squares with a sharp knife, following the lines scored into the pastry before baking. Lift out pieces with a spatula and serve hot or warm.

Serves 10 to 12

ASSEMBLING THE TYRÓPITA

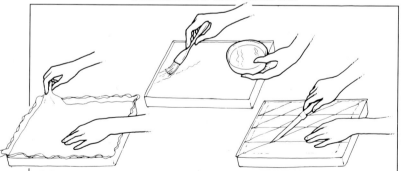

1. Line the bottom of the tin with five to six sheets of phýllo, brushing each sheet liberally with butter. **2.** Cut all but five cm of phýllo and roll over to form edging around the pie. Brush with melted butter. **3.** Score the top layers of phýllo into squares. Sprinkle with cold water. **4.** Bake until golden brown. Let cool for 15 minutes, then cut into squares.

Lamian Tyrópita

Τυρόπιτα Λαμίας

Filling
250 g (8 oz) kaséri or Gouda cheese, coarsely grated
250 g (8 oz) féta cheese, coarsely grated
250 g (8 oz) Gruyère cheese, coarsely grated
4 eggs, lightly beaten
½ liter (2 cups) milk
Salt and freshly ground black pepper
¼ tsp nutmeg
Pastry
500 g (1 lb) phýllo pastry
175 g (6 oz) melted butter or margarine

Combine the cheeses. Place 4 sheets of phýllo on the bottom of a 30 cm (12 in) round baking tin, brushing each sheet liberally with melted butter. Sprinkle the cheeses over the pastry and top with 5 to 6 sheets of phýllo, again brushing each sheet liberally with melted butter.
Cut off any excess pastry and make an attractive edge with what remains. Beat together the eggs and milk and season with salt, black pepper and nutmeg. Score the pie into squares and pour the egg mixture over it. Sprinkle with a few tablespoons of melted butter and set aside for two hours, or overnight in the refrigerator.
Bake in a moderate oven preheated to 190°C (375°F) for one hour, or until the top is golden browned. Serve hot.
Serves 10

Meat Pie with Phýllo Pastry

Κρεατόπιτα

Filling
1 kg (2 lb) ground beef, veal or lamb
3 medium onions, finely chopped
90 g (6 tbsp) butter
2 medium-sized tomatoes, halved, seeded and grated,
skins discarded
4 tbsp finely chopped parsley
Salt and freshly ground black pepper
½ tsp cinnamon (optional)
200 g (2 cups) breadcrumbs
½ liter (2 cups) milk
4 eggs, lightly beaten
125 g (1 cup) grated Parmesan cheese
Pastry
500 g (1 lb) phýllo pastry
175 g (6 oz) melted butter or margarine

To prepare the filling, sauté the meat and onions in the butter for 10 minutes. Add the tomatoes and parsley and simmer for 30 minutes more, or until the liquid has evaporated. Season the mixture with salt, pepper and cinnamon, and let cool.
Soak the breadcrumbs in the milk for 10 minutes. Squeeze out excess liquid. Combine them with the eggs and the cheese, add to the meat mixture, and reseason if necessary.
To assemble the pie, proceed as for Tyrópita (page 54).
Serves 10 to 12

Leek Pie

Πρασόπιτα

Filling

1 kg (2 lb) leeks, white parts only, finely sliced, washed and drained
30 g (2 tbsp) butter
125 g (1 cup) grated feta cheese
125 g (1 cup) grated kephalotyri, Gruyère or Parmesan cheese
5 eggs, lightly beaten
Salt and freshly ground black pepper
⅛ tsp nutmeg

Pastry

500 g (1 lb) phýllo pastry
175 g (6 oz) melted butter or margarine

For the filling, sauté the leeks in the butter until soft; let them cool. Combine the cheeses, stir in the eggs, then add the cooled leeks and season with salt, pepper and nutmeg.

To assemble the pie, proceed as for Tyrópita (page 54).

Serves 8 to 10

Onion Pie

Κρεμμυδόπιτα

The onions take on a rather sweet flavor which is enhanced by the raisins. The combination of sweet and savory is unusual in Greek cuisine.

Filling
6 medium-sized onions, thinly sliced
4 tbsp olive oil
Salt and freshly ground black pepper
150 g (1 cup) fine semolina (cream of wheat)
250 g (8 oz) féta cheese, roughly chopped
60 g (½ cup) grated kephalotýri or Parmesan cheese
3 medium-sized tomatoes, peeled and sliced
3 eggs, lightly beaten
75 g (½ cup) seedless raisins or sultánas, optional
Pastry
500 g (1 lb) phýllo pastry
¼ liter (1 cup) olive oil

Mix the onions with the olive oil and season with salt and pepper. Add the semolina, cheeses, tomatoes, eggs and raisins, and reseason if necessary.

To assemble the pie, proceed as for Tyrópita (page 54), brushing the pastry with olive oil rather than melted butter.

Serves 8 to 10

Chicken Pie

Κοτόπιτα

This is an old family recipe passed down from my mother-in-law. A chicken pie requires its own freshly cooked chickens; no leftovers here! Make sure that the filling mixture is not too runny; add more grated cheese if necessary.

Filling
2 1.5 kg (3 lb) chickens
1 kg (2 lb) onions, coarsely chopped
¼ liter (1 cup) chicken stock, or 2 bouillon cubes dissolved
in ¼ liter (1 cup) hot water
125 g (1 cup) grated kephalotýri, pecorino or Parmesan cheese
6 eggs, lightly beaten
Salt and freshly ground black pepper
¼ tsp nutmeg
Pastry
500 g (1 lb) phýllo pastry
175 g (6 oz) melted butter or margarine

Boil the chickens and onions together in the stock for 45 minutes, or until nearly tender. Remove the chicken meat from the bones and roughly chop it.

Drain the onions very well and mix them with the grated cheese, eggs, salt, pepper and nutmeg. Stir in the chicken pieces.

To assemble the pie, proceed as for Tyrópita, page 54.

Serves 10

Pastítsio with Phýllo and Féta

Παστίτσιο με Φύλλο και Τυρί Φέτα

An unusual form of the ever popular pastítsio.

Filling
500 g (1 lb) penne or other macaroni
60 g (4 tbsp) butter
500 g (1 lb) hard féta cheese, grated
5 eggs, beaten
12 cl (½ cup) milk
Salt and freshly ground black pepper
½ tsp sugar
Pastry
500 g (1 lb) phýllo pastry
175 g (6 oz) melted butter or margarine

Boil the macaroni in plenty of salted water until *al dente*. Drain, rinse lightly, and mix in the butter. Cover and set aside. In a bowl, combine the féta, eggs and milk; season with salt, pepper and sugar.

Line a large ring mold with 5 sheets of phýllo, brushing each sheet liberally with the melted butter. Layer with half of the macaroni, then the féta mixture, and top with the remaining macaroni. Cover with another 5 sheets of phýllo, buttering each sheet.

Bake in an oven preheated to 190°C (375°F) for about 1 hour, or until deliciously browned.

Let cool slightly and turn over onto a large serving dish.

Serves 12

Soldier's Pastítsio

Παστίτσιο με Φύλλο και Κιμά

Filling
500 g (1 lb) bucatini, long hollow macaroni
750 g (1½ lb) ground beef or veal
90 g (6 tbsp) butter
125 g (1 cup) grated kephalotýri or Parmesan cheese
2 eggs, beaten
1 medium-sized onion, finely chopped
12 cl (½ cup) dry red wine
750 g (1½ lb) ripe tomatoes, halved, seeded and grated,
skins discarded
1 stick cinnamon
Salt and freshly ground pepper
½ tsp sugar
Pastry
500 g (1 lb) phýllo pastry
175 g (6 oz) melted butter or margarine

Boil the macaroni in plenty of salted water until just done. Drain, rinse
and return to the saucepan. Stir in half of the butter, half of the cheese
and the eggs. Cover and set aside.

Sauté the onion in the remaining butter, add the chopped meat and simmer until all the liquid has evaporated. Add the wine and stir well; add
the tomatoes and cinnamon. Simmer slowly until all the liquid evaporates again. Season with salt, pepper and sugar.

Line a buttered baking dish 30 by 45 cm (12 by 18 in), with 5 sheets of
phýllo, brushing each sheet liberally with the melted butter. Let the excess pastry hang over the edge of the dish. Layer with one-third of the
macaroni, then half of the meat sauce. Repeat the layers, then top with
the remaining macaroni. Fold the phýllo over the filling and brush with
melted butter. Top with 5 more sheets of phýllo, again buttering each
sheet liberally. Trim the phýllo with scissors, and score with a sharp
knife into squares.

Bake in an oven preheated to 190°C (375°F) for 40 minutes to one
hour, or until the top browns.

Serves 12

Rice Pie

Ρυζόπιτα

Filling
250 g (2 cups) short grain rice, boiled, strained and rinsed
5 eggs, lightly beaten
250 g (8 oz) grated kephalotýri or Gruyère cheese
1 tbsp butter, melted
Salt and freshly ground black pepper
Pastry
500 g (1 lb) phýllo pastry
¼ liter (1 cup) olive oil

Combine the rice, eggs, cheese and butter; season with salt and pepper. To assemble the pie proceed as for Tyrópita (page 54), substituting
olive oil for melted butter.

Serves 8 to 10

Spanakópita

Σπανακόπιτα

Filling
1 kg (2 lb) spinach, washed and coarsely chopped
2 medium-sized onions, finely chopped
4 green onions, finely chopped
12 cl (½ cup) olive oil
4 tbsp finely chopped dill or parsley
4 eggs, lightly beaten
250 g (8 oz) féta cheese, coarsely grated
2 tbsp grated kephalotýri or Parmesan cheese
Salt and freshly ground black pepper
⅛ tsp nutmeg
½ tsp sugar
Pastry
500 g (1 lb) phýllo pastry
175 g (6 oz) melted butter (or half olive oil and half butter)

To make the spinach filling, heat the oil in a large saucepan, and slowly sauté the onions until transparent. Add the spinach and dill (or parsley). Continue cooking, stirring often, until the spinach is tender and all the liquid has evaporated, about 20 minutes. Set aside to cool. In a bowl, combine the eggs and the cheeses and stir in the spinach mixture. Season the filling with salt, pepper, nutmeg and sugar. Be careful not to add too much salt as the féta itself is rather salty.

To assemble the pie, proceed as for Tyrópita (page 54).

Serves 8 to 10

Zucchini Pie

Κολοκυθόπιτα

Filling
1 kg (2 lb) zucchini, scraped and grated, salted for 30 minutes
and squeezed to remove moisture
2 medium-sized onions, finely chopped
30 g (2 tbsp) butter
250 g (8 oz) féta cheese, chopped
2 tbsp grated kephalotýri or Parmesan cheese
4 eggs, lightly beaten
5 tbsp milk
1 tbsp fine semolina (cream of wheat)
4 tbsp finely chopped dill or parsley
1 tbsp chopped fresh basil (optional)
Salt and freshly ground black pepper
¼ tsp nutmeg
Pastry
500 g (1 lb) phýllo pastry
175 g (6 oz) melted butter or margarine, or a combination of the two

To prepare the filling, simmer the onions in 10 cl (½ cup) of water for 15 minutes, or until the liquid has evaporated. Add the butter and cook another 10 minutes. Add the zucchini to the onions and stir in the rest of the filling ingredients.

To assemble the pie, proceed as for Tyrópita (page 54).

Serves 8 to 10

Eggplant Pie

Μελιτζανόπιτα

This pie is particularly popular among Greeks from Egypt.

Filling
1.5 kg (3 lb) eggplant, peeled and cut in egg-size cubes
3 medium-sized onions, sliced
12 cl (½ cup) water
30 g (2 tbsp) butter
6 eggs
500 g (1 lb) grated cheese of various kinds:
Gruyère, kaseri, Emmenthal, Parmesan or kephalotýri
Salt and freshly ground black pepper
Pastry
500 g (1 lb) phýllo pastry
175 g (6 oz) melted butter or margarine, or a combination of the two

Begin this pie on the day before you need it. Simmer the onions in the water for five minutes, then add the eggplant and simmer 30 minutes more, until tender. Transfer the mixture to a colander and leave it to drain overnight. The next day pass the mixture through a food mill using the coarse blade, or briefly purée in a food processor.
Melt the butter in a frying pan and sauté the eggplant mixture in it for 15 minutes, stirring constantly, until all the liquid has evaporated. Transfer the mixture to a bowl and let it cool. Beat and add 4 eggs, ¾ of the cheese, and salt and pepper to taste.
Line a 30 by 45 cm (12 by 18 in) rectangular baking tin, or a 35 cm (14 in) round baking tin, with 5 or 6 sheets of phýllo, brushing each sheet with melted butter. Let the excess hang over the sides of the dish. Spread the eggplant mixture on top, then cover it with a sheet of phýllo. Brush the pastry with melted butter, then with beaten egg; sprinkle with ¼ of the remaining cheese. Repeat this process another four times, and top with a layer of phýllo.
Trim off all but 5 cm (2 in) of the excess phýllo with kitchen scissors and fold in the remaining pastry to make an edging. Brush the edging with melted butter. With a sharp knife, score the top layers of the pie into squares and sprinkle with a few tsp of cold water.
Bake in an oven preheated to 190° C (375° F) until golden brown, or about one hour. Serve hot or at room temperature.
Serves 10 to 12

Small Tyrópitas

Τυροπιτάκια

These are much more simple to prepare than one would assume. They are delicious finger food for children and wonderful with drinks.

Filling
500 g (1 lb) féta cheese, grated
3 tbsp grated kephalotýri or Parmesan cheese
3 tbsp finely chopped parsley
1 tbsp flour
½ tsp sugar
Pinch nutmeg
Salt and black pepper
2 tbsp milk
Pastry
500 g (1 lb) phýllo pastry
175 g (6 oz) melted butter or margarine

Combine the ingredients for the filling, adding enough milk so that the mixture has the consistency of mashed potato.

Before unrolling the phýllo, cut it into 5 cm (2 in) sections. Work with one section at a time. Unroll it, carefully separate the layers, and brush each individual layer with melted butter.

Place a teaspoon of filling at the corner of each strip of phýllo and fold up the pastry like a flag, into small triangles. Brush the tyrópitas on all sides with more melted butter. Arrange them on a baking sheet and bake in an oven preheated to 190°C (375°F) for 20 minutes, or until golden brown.

Meat Pies: To prepare a meat filling, sauté 500 g (1 lb) ground meat with 1 chopped onion. Season well with salt and pepper.

Spinach-Cheese Pies: For spinach and cheese filling, combine 250 g (1 cup) of boiled chopped spinach with 250 g (8 oz) of grated cheese.

Chicken Pies: To make small chicken pies, combine 150 g (1 cup) of chopped leftover chicken, and 4 tbsp grated cheese. Bind with 25 cl (1 cup) of thick béchamel sauce (page 42).

Makes about 50 pies

ASSEMBLING SMALL PITAS

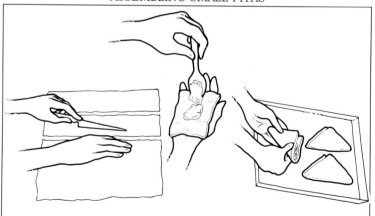

1. Cut the phýllo into 5 cm sections. **2.** Carefully unroll each section, separate the layers and brush each with melted butter. **3.** Place a teaspoon of filling at the corner of each strip and fold up like a flag.

Homemade Phýllo Pastry

Σπιτικό Φύλλο

Homemade phýllo can never be as perfect as the commercially produced pastry, but this is very good.

500 g (4 cups) flour
1 tsp salt
1½ tbsp olive oil
1 tsp vinegar or lemon juice
35 cl (1½ cups) water

Sift the flour and salt into a bowl. Make a well in the center and pour in the olive oil, vinegar (or lemon juice), and water. Mix well. The dough should be pliable. Cover and let it rest in the refrigerator for one hour. Divide the dough into quarters. On a well-floured surface, or on one that has been liberally sprinkled with cornstarch (cornflour), roll out each quarter until it is large enough to fit a 30 cm (12 in) round baking tin, with enough excess to make an attractive edging. Brush each layer of the pastry liberally with olive oil as you use it.

See the following recipes for filling ideas.

Makes one 30 cm (12 inch) pie

Small Eggplant Pies

Μελιτζανοπιτάκια

Filling
500 g (1 lb) eggplant
2 eggs, lightly beaten
125 g (1 cup) grated féta cheese
60 g (½ cup) grated kephalotýri or Parmesan cheese
Salt and freshly ground black pepper
Pastry
500 g (1 lb) phýllo pastry
175 g (6 oz) melted butter or margarine

Bake the eggplant in a moderate 190°C (375°F) oven until soft, about one hour. Remove the flesh, mash it well, strain and cool. When cooled, add the eggs and cheeses and season with salt and pepper.

To shape the small pies, proceed as on page 62.

Makes about 50 pies

Potato Pie

Πατατόπιτα

A humble but amazingly tasty pie.

Filling
6 medium-sized potatoes, thinly sliced
1 leek or onion, finely chopped
4 tbsp finely chopped parsley
3 tbsp olive oil
2 tbsp flour
Salt and freshly ground black pepper
Pastry
1 recipe homemade phýllo pastry (page 64)
12 cl (½ cup) olive oil

Combine all the ingredients for the filling. Place 2 sheets of homemade phýllo pastry in the bottom of a 30 cm (12 in) round tin, brushing
each one with olive oil. Spread the filling on top and cover with another
2 sheets of phýllo, again brushing each sheet with olive oil.
Trim the edges if necessary, and bake in an oven preheated to 190°C
(375°F) for one hour, or until the pie is golden brown.
Serves 6

Leek and Rice Pie

Πρασορυζόπιτα

Filling
500 g (1 lb) leeks, finely sliced, washed and drained
100 g (½ cup) rice, boiled for 15 minutes and strained
250 g (2 cups) grated féta or kephalotýri cheese
3 eggs, beaten
½ liter (2 cups) milk
125 g (½ cup) yogurt
12 cl (½ cup) olive oil or melted butter
Pastry
1 recipe homemade phýllo pastry
12 cl (½ cup) olive oil

Combine all the ingredients for the filling.
Place one sheet of the phýllo on the bottom of a 30 cm (12 in) round
baking tin, brush liberally with olive oil, and spread with ⅓ of the filling.
Repeat the process twice more, then top with the remaining piece of
phýllo. Brush the top layer with olive oil and score it into squares.
Bake in a moderate oven, preheated to 190°C (375°F), for one hour, or
until the pie is golden brown.
Serves 10

Savoury Pumpkin Pie

Πίτα από Κολοκύθα

This could, of course, be made with commercially produced phýllo pastry.

Filling
½ medium-sized pumpkin, or 500 g (16 oz) tinned pumpkin
1 medium-sized onion, finely chopped
125 g (4 oz) butter, melted
200 g (1 cup) rice
¼ liter (1 cup) milk
¼ liter (1 cup) water
2 tbsp finely chopped parsley
Salt and freshly ground black pepper
4 eggs, lightly beaten
250 g (2 cups) grated kephalotýri or Parmesan cheese
½ tsp cinnamon
Pastry
1 recipe homemade phýllo pastry (page 64)
12 cl (½ cup) olive oil

After removing the seeds and the fibrous parts, grate the inside of the
pumpkin. Discard the skin. Boil it for 10 minutes and strain well.
Sauté the onion in 2 tbsp of the butter until transparent. Add the pumpkin, rice, milk, water, parsley, salt and pepper and simmer for 20 minutes, until the rice is cooked. Let cool, then mix in the eggs, cheese, the
remaining butter and cinnamon.
To assemble, proceed as for Potato Pie, page 65.
Serves 10

Cheese and Garlic Soufflé Marinos

Τυρί και Σκόρδο Πουτίγγα

125 g (1 cup) grated féta cheese
125 g (1 cup) grated Gruyère cheese
3 garlic cloves, finely chopped
200 g (2 cups) fresh breadcrumbs
35 cl (1½ cup) milk
1 tbsp finely chopped basil, mint, parsley or dill
3 eggs, 1 whole and 2 separated
Salt and freshly ground black pepper

In a bowl, combine the cheeses, garlic, breadcrumbs, milk, basil, 1
whole egg and two egg yolks. Mix well and season with salt and pepper. Beat the remaining 2 egg whites until stiff and fold them into the
breadcrumb mixture.
Transfer the mixture to a buttered 20 cm (8 in) soufflé dish and bake in
a hot oven preheated to 220°C (425°F), for 40 minutes. Serve with a
tomato salad.
Serves 4

Cheese Soufflé

Σουφλέ από Τυρί

Much simpler to prepare than a true soufflé, this is popular with children and easy to serve on a buffet table.

300 g (10 oz) kaseri, Gruyère or Emmenthal cheese, coarsely grated
1 small loaf white bread, crusts removed then frozen
60 gr (4 tbsp) butter
6 slices ham, chopped
5 eggs, well beaten
1 liter (4 cups) milk

Freezing the bread will make it easier to work with. Butter the bread slices on one side. Layer half of the bread on the bottom of a buttered baking dish, 24 by 36 cm (10 by 14 in). Sprinkle with the ham and half of the cheese. Layer the remaining bread on top, and cover with the remaining cheese.

Combine the eggs and milk and pour them over the bread. Refrigerate for at least 1 hour, or overnight if it is more convenient. Bake in an oven preheated to 190°C (375°F), for 45 minutes, or until golden brown.

Serves 6 to 8

Tyrópita without Pastry

Τυρόπιτα χωρίς Φύλλο

A very quick and easy recipe, this is excellent for a summer buffet, or to serve with drinks.

250 g (8 oz) féta cheese, roughly chopped
125 g (4 oz) Gruyère cheese, roughly chopped
125 g (1 cup) flour
225 g (1 cup) yogurt
125 g (4 oz) butter, melted
3 eggs, beaten
½ tsp baking soda

Combine all the ingredients and mix well. Transfer to a 22 cm (9 in) round buttered baking dish. Bake in an oven preheated to 190°C (375°F) for about 35 minutes, or until brown. Cut into small squares and serve warm.

Serves 8

Féta Cheese Bread

Τυρόψωμο

500 g (1 lb) féta cheese, roughly chopped
500 g (4 cups) flour
2 tsp baking powder
4 eggs, beaten
½ liter (2 cups) milk
75 g (5 tbsp) melted butter

With the exception of 1 tbsp of the butter, combine all the ingredients, mix well and transfer to a 22 cm (9 in) round buttered baking tin. Sprinkle the remaining butter on top. Bake in an oven preheated to 190°C (375°F) until golden brown, about 25 minutes. Serve warm.

Serves 8

Onion Bread

Κρεμμυδόψωμο

6 green onions or 1 large onion, finely chopped
7 g (¼ oz) dried yeast
12 cl (½ cup) warm water
12 cl (½ cup) olive oil
3 eggs
Salt and freshly ground black pepper
250 g (2 cups) flour
3 tbsp finely chopped dill
125 g (4 oz) féta cheese, crumbled

To prepare the dough, dissolve the yeast in warm water for three to five minutes. Stir in 1 tbsp of the olive oil, 1 egg, salt and pepper. Combine with the flour and knead for five minutes. Cover the dough with a cloth and leave it to rise in a warm place until it has doubled in volume, about two hours.

Meanwhile, sauté the onions in the remaining olive oil until soft and transparent; add the dill and let cool. When the onion mixture has cooled, beat the two remaining eggs and add them to it. Season with salt and pepper. Divide the dough in half. Roll out one piece to fit the bottom of a well-oiled 22 cm (9 in) round baking tin. Sprinkle with the féta and the onion mixture. Roll out the other half of the dough and put it on top. Score the top layer into squares and brush liberally with some additional olive oil. Bake in a hot oven preheated to 220°C (425°F) for 25 to 30 minutes, or until golden brown. Serve with *mezés* or a buffet luncheon.

Serves 8

Sfoliáta Pastry

Σπιτική Σφολιάτα

According to the size of your eggs or the consistency of your yogurt, you may need to vary the amount of water or wine used.

500 g (4 cups) flour
24 cl (1 cup) olive oil
1 tsp salt
2 eggs, or 200 g (1 cup) yogurt
4 tbsp water, or white wine

Combine the flour, olive oil, salt, and eggs (or yogurt). Mix in enough water to make a soft dough. Let it rest in the refrigerator for 2 hours. Divide the dough in half and roll out on a well-floured surface. See the following recipes for filling ideas.

Sufficient for top and bottom of a 30 cm (12 in) pie.

Kaltsoúnia

Καλτσούνια

This is a Cretan recipe which is traditionally made at Easter. On a visit to Crete, I was surprised to see spinach hanging out to dry on clothes lines, waiting to be chopped and stuffed into Kaltsoúnia.

1 kg (2 lb) spinach, stems removed, washed, dried and finely chopped
500 g (1 lb) mizíthra or cottage cheese
500 g (4 cups) flour
2 tbsp olive oil
30 cl (1¼ cup) water
1 egg, beaten
3 tbsp sesame seeds

Combine the spinach and cheese and mix well.
To make the pastry, combine the flour, olive oil and enough water to form a fairly stiff dough. Roll it out quite thinly on a floured surface, and cut into 10 cm (4 in) circles. Place 1 tbsp of the spinach mixture on each circle, fold in half and pinch the edges together.
Fry in hot oil until golden brown. Kaltsoúnia are best eaten hot, but may also be served at room temperature.
Variation: Fill the pies with plain cottage cheese or mizíthra, or cheese mixed with chopped mint, or with seasoned chopped meat. One may also bake rathern fry the kaltsoúnia but then they should be brushed with heaven egg and sprinkled with sesame seeds.
Makes 45 pies

Meat Pie with Sfoliáta

Κρεατόπιτα

Filling
500 g (1 lb) ground beef or veal
2 medium-sized onions, finely sliced
2 tbsp butter
Salt and freshly ground black pepper
½ tsp cinnamon
2 eggs, separated
25 cl (1 cup) béchamel sauce
125 gr (1 cup) grated kephalotýri or Gruyère cheese
2 tbsp breadcrumbs
Pastry
1 recipe sfoliáta pastry (page 69)

Sauté the onions in the butter. Add the ground beef, salt, pepper and cinnamon. Sauté for five minutes or until the liquid has evaporated, then set aside to cool.

Lightly beat the egg whites. When the meat mixture has cooled, add the béchamel sauce, 1 egg yolk, the cheese, breadcrumbs and egg whites. Divide the sfoliáta pastry in two. Roll out one half and use it to line the bottom of a 30 cm (12 in) baking tin. Spread the meat mixture over it. Roll out the rest of the pastry and place it on top of the pie. Brush with the remaining egg yolk. Bake in an oven preheated to 190°C (375°F) for 35 minutes, or until golden brown.

Serves 10

Lamb Pie

Πίτα αρνιού

Filling
1 kg (2 lb) leg of lamb, cut into 2 cm (1 in) cubes
5 green onions, sliced
60 g (4 tbsp) butter
3 tbsp finely chopped dill
Salt and freshly ground black pepper
¼ liter (1 cup) warm water
60 g (½ cup) grated kaséri cheese
60 g (½ cup) grated kephalotýri or Parmesan cheese
2 eggs, beaten
Pastry
1 recipe sfoliáta pastry (page 69)
1 egg yolk

Sauté the lamb and green onions in the butter for 10 minutes. Add the dill, salt, pepper and the water. Simmer until the lamb is tender, approximately 30 minutes. If necessary, add more warm water to prevent sticking. Cool the meat mixture, then add the cheeses and eggs.

To assemble, proceed as for Meat Pie with Sfoliáta, above.

Makes one 30 cm (12 inch) pie

Cephalonian Meat Pie

Κεφαλονίτικη Πίτα

This is a very old recipe, and unsual in that it contains prunes.

Filling
1 kg (2 lb) lean lamb or beef, cut into 2 cm (1 in) cubes
1 medium-sized onion, finely chopped
60 g (4 tbsp) olive oil and butter
12 cl (½ cup) wine
12 cl (½ cup) tomato juice
100 g (½ cup) rice
2 hardboiled eggs, quartered
100 g (1 cup) cubed cheese: kephalotyri, Gruyère or Parmesan
8 prunes, stoned and chopped
2 tbsp pine nuts
1 clove garlic, finely chopped
50 g (1 cup) finely chopped dill
50 g (1 cup) finely chopped parsley
Salt and freshly ground black pepper

Pastry
1 recipe sfoliáta pastry (page 69)

Sauté the meat and onion in the oil and butter until the onion is transparent and the meat is browned. Add the wine, the tomato juice and all the other ingredients. Season with salt and pepper and set aside.

Next, prepare the sfoliáta pastry according to the recipe.

Line a 30 cm (12 in) baking tin with half of the pastry. Spread the filling over and top with the other half of the pastry.

Bake in an oven pre-heated to 190°C (375°F) for one hour.

Serves 10 to 12

Mykonian Onion Pie

Κρεμμυδόπιτα

Filling
500 g (1 lb) feta cheese, crumbled (or half féta and half cottage cheese)
6 green onions, finely chopped
3 eggs
2 tbsp finely chopped dill
1 tbsp lemon juice
Salt and freshly ground black pepper

Pastry
1 recipe sfoliáta pastry (page 69)
6 cl (¼ cup) olive oil

Combine the filling ingredients in a bowl.

Roll out half the pastry and use it to line a 30 cm (12 in) round baking tin. Brush liberally with olive oil, then spread the filling mixture over. Roll out the remaining pastry and put it on top. Brush liberally with the remaining olive oil.

Bake in a moderate oven, preheated to 190°C (375°F) for one hour, or until the pie is browned.

Serves 10

Vegetables

Artichokes à la Políta

Αγκινάρες α λα Πολίτα

Artichokes à la Políta, cooked in the style of Constantinople, is one of the outstanding dishes in Greek cuisine. The Greeks of Asia Minor, and particularly those from Constantinople, are reputed to be among the best cooks in the land, and have earned the reputation with recipes such as this one.

Wild artichokes grow all over Greece, and if you have the patience and can bear the spikes, you may enjoy gathering, cleaning, boiling and then eating them with salt.

Since fresh dill is truly far superior to dried dill for any purpose whatsoever, it is best to find a source. Or grow your own, which is quite easy to do from seeds sown in the spring. Dried dill will provide an acceptable visual substitute, if it is all you can find.

12 artichokes, 5 cm (2 in) of stalks left on
you may substitute frozen artichoke hearts if fresh are unavailable
6 green onions, finely chopped
12 small onions, peeled
4 medium-sized carrots, peeled and sliced crosswise
3 medium-sized potatoes, peeled and cut in eighths
2 tbsp finely chopped dill
3 tbsp flour
4 tbsp lemon juice
12 cl (½ cup) olive oil
¾ liter (3 cups) water
Salt and pepper

To get to the heart of the artichoke, remove the tough outer leaves, cut off about 3 cm (1 in) from the top of the remaining leaves, and scoop out the fuzzy choke inside. Peel the tough outer skin of the stalks. Immediately put the artichokes in a bowl of cold water with 1 tbsp flour and 1 tbsp lemon juice, so that they do not discolor.

Cover the bottom of a large saucepan with the green onions, whole onions, carrots, artichokes, and finally potatoes. Sprinkle with dill.

Combine the remaining 2 tbsp flour, 3 tbsp lemon juice, olive oil, water, salt and pepper. Pour this mixture over the artichokes.

Cover the saucepan and simmer very slowly for 40 minutes to an hour, or until the artichokes are tender. Serve warm or at room temperature, for a first course or a light luncheon dish.

Serves 6

CLEANING THE ARTICHOKES

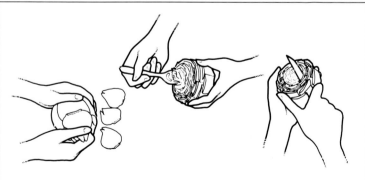

1. Break off the tough outer leaves. Cut off about 3 cm from the top of the remaining leaves. **2.** Scoop out the fuzzy choke inside. **3.** With a knife, take away any dark green parts from the top and bottom of the artichoke and stalk.

Broad Beans Yahní

Κουκιά Γιαχνί

Look for broad beans, "koukiá" in Greek, in Mediterranean food shops or health food stores. Their earthy flavor is appealing in its simplicity.

1 kg (2 lb) broad beans, shelled, or 500 g (1 lb) frozen
3 green onions, finely chopped
12 cl (½ cup) olive oil
¾ liter (3 cups) water
2 tbsp finely chopped dill or parsley
Salt and freshly ground black pepper
1 lemon, juice only

Sauté the green onions for five minutes in the olive oil. Add the broad beans, dill (or parsley), and cover with the water. Simmer for 30 minutes, or until the broad beans are tender and most of the liquid has evaporated. Season with salt, black pepper and the lemon juice. Serve hot or at room temperature, garnished with lemon wedges.
Variation: Use half broad beans and half fresh peas.

Serves 4

Butter Beans Plakí

Φασόλια Γίγαντες Πλακί

For best results, try to find "fasólia gígantes" in a Mediterranean grocery, as butter beans aren't quite the same. This vegetarian dish is rich and filling, and is one of the highlights of Greek cuisine. It is a favorite served with a selection of mezés, at home or in a taverna.

500 g (1 lb) large butter beans, soaked overnight and drained
1 medium-sized onion, finely chopped
12 cl (½ cup) olive oil
6 medium-sized tomatoes, halved, seeded and grated,
skins discarded
2 carrots, peeled and sliced
3 celery sticks, finely chopped
25 g (½ cup) finely chopped parsley
¼ liter (1 cup) dry red wine
Salt and freshly ground black pepper
½ tsp sugar

In a heavy saucepan, cover the butter beans with cold unsalted water and simmer until tender, about 1½ hours. Drain and rinse them immediately, so that the outside skins do not split. Cover them with cold water and reserve until needed.

Sauté the onion in the olive oil until transparent, then add the tomatoes, carrots, celery, parsley and wine. Simmer for 30 minutes, or until the vegetables are tender. Season with salt, pepper and sugar.

Gently combine the beans and vegetables. Bake them in a large shallow baking dish for 30 minutes, in an oven preheated to 190°C (375°F).
Serve hot or warm.

Serves 8

Cauliflower Kapamá

Κουνουπίδι Καπαμάς

A tasty recipe, kapamá may also be served with a variety of mezés.

1 kg (2 lb) cauliflower, divided into bite-sized florets
1 lemon, juice strained
3 medium-sized tomatoes, halved, seeded and grated,
skins discarded
12 cl (½ cup) olive oil
½ to 1 tsp cinnamon
½ tsp sugar
Salt and freshly ground black pepper
Chopped parsley

Put the cauliflower florets in a bowl and sprinkle with the lemon juice. Let marinate for five minutes, then drain.

Heat the oil in a saucepan until it smokes. Toss in the cauliflower and sauté for 10 minutes, stirring. Reduce the heat and add the tomatoes, cinnamon, sugar, salt and pepper. Cover and simmer for 30 minutes, or until the cauliflower is tender. Shake the saucepan occasionally and if necessary, add a little hot water, to prevent sticking. Garnish with lots of chopped parsley and serve with keftedákia (page 135).

Serves 6

Cabbage and Celery Avgolémono

Λάχανο με Σέλινο Αυγολέμονο

This vegetarian dish compliments roast pork, and is generally served in the winter months when cabbage and celery are available.

500 g (1 lb) cabbage, roughly chopped
500 g (1 lb) celery, chopped
1 large onion, finely chopped
12 cl (½ cup) olive oil
3 medium-sized tomatoes, halved, seeded and grated,
skins discarded
½ hot red pepper, finely chopped
Salt and freshly ground black pepper
½ tsp sugar
1 egg
1 lemon, juice only

In a saucepan sauté the onion in the olive oil until transparent. Add the cabbage and sauté for five minutes, until it softens. Next, add the tomatoes, celery and red pepper; season with salt, pepper and sugar. Simmer for 30 minutes, or until the vegetables are tender.

In a bowl beat the egg well. Slowly add the lemon juice and most of the liquid from the saucepan, stirring constantly. Gradually pour the egg mixture back into the saucepan, continuing to stir. If necessary, reheat slowly, uncovered and without boiling.

Serves 4 to 6

Chick Peas with Onions

Ρεβίθια με Κρεμμύδια

This recipe comes from Siphnos. Traditionally, chick peas are cooked slowly overnight in the leftover heat of the local baker's oven. They are cooked in shallow round earthenware "youvétsi" pots, and the baker adds rainwater to prevent sticking –a rather difficult process to duplicate at home! Many Greeks still use the baker's oven to cook a roast or casserole. Not only does the house stay cooler in the summer months, but the heat of the large ovens and the baker's experience often add a great deal of flavor to the end result.

500 g (1 lb) chick peas, soaked overnight in cold water and drained
1 tbsp baking soda
3 medium-sized onions, finely chopped
4 tbsp olive oil
3 medium-sized tomatoes, halved, seeded and grated,
skins discarded
Salt and freshly ground black pepper
½ tsp sugar

If the chick peas you are using are not preskinned, follow this proce-dure to remove skins. Sprinkle the chick peas with the baking soda and stir. Let them stand for 15 minutes, then wash well with hot water; drain. Taking a handful at a time, place the chick peas on a cloth and rub to remove the skins. Rinse well and transfer them to a round covered oven-proof dish.

Sauté the onions in 3 tbsp of olive oil until transparent; spread them over the chick peas. Simmer together the tomatoes, 1 tbsp olive oil, pepper and sugar for 20 minutes, or until they thicken. Pour over the chick peas. Cover and bake in a preheated 150°C (300°F) oven until the chick peas are tender, about two hours. If necessary, add a little hot water occasionally to prevent sticking. Season with salt before serving.

Serves 6

Eggplant Croquettes

Μελιτζανοκεφτέδες

1 kg (2 lb) eggplant
60 g (½ cup) grated kephalotýri or Parmesan cheese
150 g (1½ cup) breadcrumbs
1 tsp baking powder
2 eggs
2 tbsp finely chopped parsley
1 tbsp finely chopped onion
Salt and freshly ground black pepper
Breadcrumbs
Olive oil for deep-frying

Prick the eggplant all over and either broil or bake for 30 minutes, until tender. Discard the skins and seeds, too, if large. In a bowl, mash the eggplant. Mix in the cheese, breadcrumbs, baking powder, eggs, pars-ley and onion. Season with salt and pepper.

Shape the mixture into five cm (2 in) croquettes and roll them in bread-crumbs. Refrigerate the croquettes for at least one hour, then deep-fry in olive oil until well browned. Drain on paper towels and serve hot.

Serves 6 to 8

Mediterranean Vegetable Croquettes

Λαχανοκεφτέδες

1 kg (2 lb) zucchini, coarsely grated
1 medium-sized eggplant, coarsely grated
1 green pepper, coarsely grated
1 large potato, coarsely grated
1 large onion, coarsely grated
4 tbsp (¼ cup) finely chopped parsley
1 tbsp finely chopped mint
¼ tsp cayenne pepper
¼ tsp black pepper
125 gr (4 oz) féta cheese
4 tbsp grated kephalotýri or Parmesan cheese
2 eggs
50 g (½ cup) dry breadcrumbs
Flour
Olive oil for frying

Combine all the ingredients except the flour and olive oil. Add enough breadcrumbs to make a stiff mixture, and refrigerate it for at least one hour. Form the mixture into patties. Roll them in flour and sauté in 2 cm (1 in) of olive oil, or deep-fry until golden.
Drain on paper towels and serve hot.
Serves 8

Eggplant and Féta Cheese Casserole

Μελιτζάνες με Τυρί Φέτα

A Mediterranean classic.

1 kg (2 lb) large eggplant, peeled and cut in 1 cm (½ in) slices
6 medium-sized tomatoes, halved, seeded and grated, skins discarded
125 g (1 cup) féta cheese, crumbled
Salt and freshly ground black pepper
½ tsp sugar
¼ liter (1 cup) olive oil for sautéing

Salt the eggplant slices liberally and leave them for one hour. Rinse with cold water and dry well.
Heat 2 cm (1 in) of olive oil in a frying pan, and in it sauté the eggplant a few slices at a time, until just golden. Add more olive oil as needed, because some will be absorbed by the eggplant. Drain the eggplant well on paper towels.
Simmer the tomatoes seasoned with salt, pepper and sugar for 25 minutes, or until they thicken. Layer a shallow ovenproof dish with half of the eggplant, cover with half of the tomato sauce and sprinkle with half of the féta. Repeat the layers. Preheat the oven to 190°C (375°F) and bake for about 25 minutes, or until the cheese bubbles and browns.
Variation: This dish is also delicious with mozzarella or Parmesan cheese rather than féta.
Serves 6 to 8

Briám

Μπριάμι

Briám is the ratatouille of Greece. It is served in summer as a main course when all the vegetables are available fresh from the garden. Vary the ingredients according to what is on hand, or try adding different ones, such as green beans or okra. Don't skimp on the olive oil, or the results will be less than delicious!

1 kg (2 lb) eggplant, unpeeled, cut in egg-size pieces
1 kg (2 lb) zucchini, unpeeled, cut crosswise into 1 cm (½ in) slices
6 medium-sized tomatoes, halved, seeded and grated,
skins discarded
3 potatoes, peeled and cut in walnut-sized pieces
3 large green peppers, seeded and sliced
3 medium-sized onions, sliced
3 garlic cloves, crushed with 1 tsp salt
¼ liter (1 cup) dry red wine
¼ liter (1 cup) olive oil
25 g (½ cup) finely chopped parsley
Several fresh basil leaves
Salt and freshly ground black pepper
½ tsp sugar

Combine all the ingredients in a large shallow ovenproof casserole or baking dish. Stirring occasionally, bake the briám in a moderate oven preheated to 190°C (375°F) for 1½ hours, or until the vegetables are tender. Add a little boiling water from time to time if necessary to prevent sticking. Serve hot or at room temperature.
Serves 8

Eggplant Imám Baildí

Μελιτζάνες Ιμάμ Μπαϊλντί

An imám is a Muslim religious leader; "baildí" means he fainted. Exactly why the imám fainted is the source of much speculation, but we are reasonably sure that it was due to both the extravagance of his chef and the richness of this dish.

Long slim eggplant are the ones to use for this recipe. The end result is eggplant stuffed with onions, their flavors mingled together under the cover of tomato slices. You may prepare the imám baildí on the day before you serve it, which will enhance the flavors.

6 long eggplant, stems left on
¼ liter (1 cup) olive oil
4 onions, 2 finely sliced and 2 finely chopped
2 or 3 garlic cloves, finely chopped
2 tbsp finely chopped parsley
Salt and freshly ground black pepper
½ tsp sugar
4 tomatoes, sliced
Breadcrumbs

With the tip of a knife, make 3 lengthwise incisions in each eggplant. Liberally sprinkle the incisions with salt and leave for 30 minutes. Wash and dry the eggplant. In half of the olive oil, sauté the eggplant on all sides for 20 minutes, or until fairly soft. Reserve the oil and drain the eggplant on paper towels.

Place the eggplant in a baking dish just large enough to hold them, and put the sliced onions between.

Sauté the chopped onions in the oil remaining in the frying pan. Add the parsley and garlic. Season with salt, pepper and sugar; mix well and cool slightly. Stuff the incisions in the eggplant with this mixture.

Place the sliced tomatoes on top of the eggplant and sprinkle them with salt, dry breadcrumbs and the remaining olive oil. Bake in an oven pre-heated to 190°C (375°F), for about one hour. Serve warm or at room temperature.

Serves 6

Macedonian Eggplant

Μακεδονίτικες Μελιτζάνες

This recipe comes from Naoussa, in Macedonia. Naoussa was the home of Philip and Alexander the Great, and is known today for its excellent red wine. This is a very tasty summer dish, best eaten at room temperature.

500 g (1 lb) eggplant, sliced as thinly as possible
6 medium-sized tomatoes, halved, seeded and grated,
skins discarded
3 tbsp finely chopped parsley
2 tbsp olive oil
3 garlic cloves, finely chopped
Salt and freshly ground black pepper
½ tsp sugar
Garlic Sauce
10 garlic cloves
8 cl (⅓ cup) wine vinegar
¼ tsp salt

Simmer together the tomatoes, parsley, olive oil, garlic, salt, pepper and sugar for about 10 minutes, or until the sauce thickens slightly. Remove the garlic.

In an ovenproof dish, make layers of sliced eggplant sprinkled with salt and tomato sauce, ending with the sauce. Bake uncovered in an oven preheated to 190°C (375°F), for 45 minutes, or until the eggplant is tender.

To prepare the garlic sauce, process or blend together the garlic, vinegar and salt. Serve in a small bowl on the side.

Serves 4

Vegetarian Moussaká

Μουσακάς χωρίς Κρέας

A tasty vegetarian alternative to traditional moussaká.

1 kg (2 lb) eggplant, cut in 1 cm (½ in) slices
10 fresh tomatoes, halved, seeded and grated, skins discarded
¼ liter (1 cup) olive oil
Salt and freshly ground black pepper
½ tsp sugar
100 g (2 cups) parsley, finely chopped
3 tbsp breadcrumbs

Salt the eggplant slices liberally and leave them for 30 minutes. Rinse and dry with paper towels.

Make a good thick sauce by simmering together the tomatoes, 3 tbsp of the olive oil, salt, pepper and sugar, for about 40 minutes.

Meanwhile, heat 2 cm (1 in) of olive oil in a frying pan and sauté the eggplant in batches until just golden. Add more oil if necessary. Drain well on paper towels.

Cover the bottom of a shallow baking dish with half of the eggplant, sprinkle with half of the parsley and pour over half of the tomato sauce. Repeat the process and top with the breadcrumbs. Bake in an oven preheated to 190°C (375°F), for about 30 minutes, or until the top browns.

Serves 6

Eggplant Smothered in Garlic

Μελιτζάνες Σκορδοστούμπι

This is a simple but delicious dish from Zakynthos.

2 kg (4 lb) large round eggplant, unpeeled, cut into
1 cm (½ in) slices
Olive oil for sautéing
8 tomatoes, halved, seeded and grated, skins discarded
Salt and freshly ground black pepper
½ tsp sugar
1 to 2 tbsp vinegar
1 head garlic, peeled, and finely chopped

Sprinkle the eggplant slices with salt and leave them for half an hour. Wash and dry.

Heat about 2 cm (1 in) of olive oil in a frying pan and gently fry the eggplant in batches, being careful not to brown them too much. Drain on absorbent paper.

In another frying pan, simmer the tomatoes seasoned with salt, pepper and sugar until they make a thick sauce. Add a little vinegar to taste.

Arrange the eggplant slices in layers in an ovenproof dish and sprinkle the garlic in between the layers. Pour the tomato sauce over the eggplant and cook in an oven pre-heated to 190°C (375°F) for about 30 minutes. This dish is best served when slightly cooled. Serve with fresh bread, feta cheese and plenty of wine.

Variation: Rather than frying the eggplant, brush the slices with olive oil on both sides and broil or grill them until tender. This will make the dish less rich. And you may substitute red wine for vinegar to achieve a more mellow flavor.

Serves 8 to 10

Eggplant Yahní

Μελιτζάνες Γιαχνί

Try using half eggplant and half zucchini for this recipe.

1 kg (2 lb) eggplant, unpeeled, cut in egg-sized chunks
2 medium-sized onions, finely chopped
6 medium-sized tomatoes, halved, seeded and grated,
skins discarded
¼ liter (1 cup) olive oil
¾ liter (3 cups) water
Salt and freshly ground black pepper
½ tsp sugar
2 tbsp finely chopped parsley

In a heavy saucepan, sauté the onions in the olive oil until golden. Add the eggplant and sauté for another five minutes. Next add the tomatoes and the water. Simmer for 40 minutes, or until the eggplant is tender and the sauce has thickened. Season with salt, pepper and sugar, and sprinkle with parsley. Traditionally, this dish is served at room temperature with féta cheese.

Serves 6

Peas Yahní

Αρακάς Γιαχνί

If you use frozen peas, cook them only about fifteen minutes, and reduce the water to 2 to 3 tablespoons.

1 kg (2 lb) fresh peas, shelled or 500 g (1 lb) frozen peas
3 green onions, finely chopped
12 cl (½ cup) olive oil
2 tbsp finely chopped dill
3 medium-sized tomatoes, halved, seeded and grated,
skins discarded
12 cl (½ cup) water
Salt and freshly ground black pepper
¼ tsp sugar

In a saucepan, sauté the green onions in the olive oil until transparent. Add the peas and dill, sauté lightly for three to four minutes, then add the tomatoes and the water. Simmer, half covered, for about 25 minutes, or until the peas are tender and most of the liquid has evaporated. Season with salt, pepper and sugar. Serve hot or at room temperature.
Variation: Omit the tomatoes, increase the water to ¼ liter (1 cup) and add the juice of 1 lemon at the end of cooking.
Serves 4

Lentils Yahní

Φακές Γιαχνί

A hearty cold weather luncheon dish.

500 g (1 lb) lentils
2 large onions, 1 whole and 1 finely chopped
1 bay leaf
Water to cover
2 green peppers, thinly sliced
2 garlic cloves, finely chopped
12 cl (½ cup) olive oil
3 medium-sized tomatoes, peeled, seeded and chopped
'Salt and freshly ground black pepper
¼ liter (1 cup) hot water

Boil the lentils with the whole onion, the bay leaf and enough water to cover for 20 minutes. Drain the lentils and discard the onion and bay leaf. Sauté the chopped onion, green pepper and garlic in the olive oil until soft. Add the tomatoes, lentils and the hot water. Simmer for about 20 minutes, or until the sauce thickens and the lentils are done. Season with salt and pepper and serve with fresh crusty bread.
Serves 5 to 6

Okra Yahní

Μπάμιες Γιαχνί

Choose the smallest and best looking okra you can find. Remove the stalk and trim around the conical head of the vegetable, being careful not to cut through to the interior chambers. (The liquid would escape and the okra would lose its shape during cooking).
In Greece, okra is usually prepared this way or combined with chicken or meat in a casserole. You may use tinned okra, strained and rinsed or frozen okra to prepare this dish. Both require less cooking time (about 10 minutes), but neither equals the flavor of the fresh vegetable.

1 kg (2 lb) okra, stalks removed and trimmed
12 cl (½ cup) wine vinegar
1 medium-sized onion, grated
12 cl (½ cup) water
12 cl (½ cup) olive oil
3 medium-sized tomatoes, halved, seeded and grated,
skins discarded
3 tbsp finely chopped parsley
Salt and freshly ground black pepper
½ tsp sugar

Spread out the okra on a tray, sprinkle with salt and the vinegar, and leave for 30 minutes to one hour, preferably in the sun. Rinse the okra well and dry it.

In a saucepan, boil the onion with the water for about five minutes, or until the water has evaporated. Add the oil and the okra and sauté for five minutes more. Then add the tomatoes and parsley, and season with salt, pepper and sugar. Simmer for about 20 minutes, or until the okra is tender and the liquid has been reduced to a thick sauce. If necessary, add a little hot water to prevent sticking. Serve the dish hot or at room temperature with féta cheese and fresh bread.

Serves 6

Black-Eyed Peas and Spinach

Μαυρομάτικα Φασόλια με Σπανάκι

250 g (½ lb) black-eyed peas
750 g (1½ lb) spinach, washed, boiled and drained
1 medium-sized onion, finely chopped
12 cl (½ cup) olive oil
3 medium-sized tomatoes, halved, seeded and grated,
skins discarded
Salt and freshly ground black pepper
½ tsp sugar

Boil the black-eyed peas in unsalted water for 30 to 40 minutes or until just tender; drain. Sauté the onion in the oil until transparent. Add the spinach, the black-eyed peas and the tomatoes.
Simmer slowly, partly covered, for 30 minutes more, or until the sauce thickens. Season with salt, pepper and sugar.
Serves 6

Cracked Potatoes

Τσακιστές Πατάτες

This is a recipe from Cyprus. Use very small new potatoes for best results.

1 kg (2 lb) small new potatoes, unpeeled but well washed
¼ liter (1 cup) olive oil
1½ tbsp crushed coriander seeds
¼ liter (1 cup) dry red wine
Salt and pepper

Bang each potato with a mallet so that it cracks open slightly. Sauté the potatoes in hot olive oil until they are browned. Discard all but 2 tbsp of the oil. Add the coriander seed to the potatoes, sauté for two to three minutes, then add the wine and season with salt and pepper. Simmer, covered, for about 20 minutes, or until the potatoes are tender. These are delicious served hot or cold.
Serves 5 to 6

Potatoes Riganáto

Πατάτες Ριγανάτες

You may reduce the oil slightly and roast the potatoes together with a chicken or leg of lamb for dramatic results! The cooking juices lend superb flavor to the lemon-flavored potatoes.

10 potatoes, peeled and quartered
¼ liter (1 cup) olive oil
2 or 3 lemons, juice only
Salt and freshly ground black pepper
2 to 3 tsp oregano

Spread out the potatoes in a dish just large enough to hold them in one layer. Pour over them the olive oil and the lemon juice. Sprinkle liberally with salt, pepper and oregano.
Bake in oven preheated to 190°C (375°F) until the potatoes are soft inside and crisp outside, about 1 hour. Stir the potatoes once or twice while cooking. Serve with roast meat or chicken.
Serves 6

Potato Croquettes

Πατατοκεφτέδες

The croquettes are delicious prepared with chopped fresh dill and green onions.

3 large potatoes, peeled
25 g (½ cup) finely chopped parsley
1 egg yolk
125 g (1 cup) grated kephalotýri, Gruyère or Parmesan cheese
Salt and freshly ground black pepper
Nutmeg
75 g (½ cup) flour
1 egg, beaten
100 g (1 cup) breadcrumbs
¼ liter (1 cup) oil for deep-frying

Boil the potatoes for 25 minutes or until soft; drain them. In a bowl, mash them well. When cool, mix in the parsley, egg yolk and cheese, and season with salt, pepper and nutmeg.

Shape the mixture into 5 cm (2 in) croquettes or walnut-sized balls. Dip them first in flour, then beaten egg, and finally in breadcrumbs. Refrigerate the croquettes for one hour, so that the breading will dry.

Deep-fry in hot oil until golden brown; drain on paper towels. Serve either with tomato sauce (page 40) or as a *mezé*.

Makes about 15 to 20 croquettes

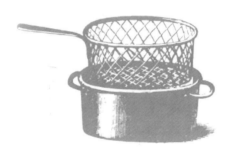

Zucchini with Féta Cheese

Κολοκυθάκια με Φέτα

A quick delightful summer dish.

1 kg (2 lb) small zucchini, lightly scraped
30 g (2 tbsp) butter
125 g (4 oz) féta cheese, cut in small pieces
Salt and freshly ground black pepper

Boil the zucchini for 15 minutes, or until just tender. Cut it into 2 cm (1 in) slices. Sauté the slices in the butter for 5 minutes, add the féta and stir well. Season with salt and pepper and serve very hot.

Serves 4

Zucchini Croquettes

Κολοκυθοκεφτέδες

1 kg (2 lb) zucchini, scraped, grated and well squeezed
125 g (1 cup) grated kephalotýri, Parmesan or pecorino cheese
100 g (1 cup) breadcrumbs
2 eggs, slightly beaten
25 g (½ cup) finely chopped parsley
4 tbsp finely chopped green onions
2 tbsp finely chopped dill or mint
Salt and freshly ground black pepper
Flour
Butter or olive oil for sautéing

Combine all the ingredients except the flour and butter (or oil). Refrigerate for one to two hours.
Shape the mixture into 5 cm (2 in) croquettes and roll them in flour. Sauté them in hot butter (or olive oil), turning gently, until golden on all sides. Serve with tomato sauce (page 40) and a salad. Makes about 24 croquettes.
Serves 4 to 6

Zucchini with Féta Cheese and Tomatoes

Κολοκυθάκια με Φέτα και Ντομάτα

1 kg (2 lb) zucchini, scraped and cut crosswise into
1 cm (½ in) slices
125 g (4 oz) féta cheese, cut in small pieces
3 medium-sized tomatoes, halved, seeded and grated,
skins discarded
1 green onion, finely chopped
1 garlic clove crushed with 1 tsp salt
12 cl (½ cup) olive oil
½ tsp sugar
Salt and freshly ground black pepper

In a large saucepan, lightly sauté the onion and garlic in the olive oil. Add the zucchini and continue cooking until it's lightly browned. Add the tomatoes and season with the sugar. Simmer for about 20 minutes until the sauce thickens. Stir in the féta and season with salt and pepper.
Serves 4 to 6

Stuffed
Vegetables

Cabbage Dolmádes

Νηστήσιμοι Λαχανοντολμάδες

1 large cabbage, parboiled for 10 minutes, rinsed, drained and leaves removed
2 medium-sized onions, finely chopped or grated
12 cl (½ cup) olive oil
200 g (1 cup) short grain rice
1 large tomato, peeled, seeded and finely chopped
4 tbsp (¼ cup) chopped parsley
1 lemon, juice only
1 tsp allspice
1 tsp ground cinnamon
Cayenne pepper to taste
Salt and freshly ground black pepper

Gently sauté the onions in several tablespoons of the olive oil for about
10 minutes. Add the rice, tomato, parsley and lemon juice, and season
with the spices, salt and pepper. Mix well.

Trim off the thick stems of the cabbage leaves. Place a tablespoon of
stuffing on each leaf and roll up, tacking in the ends. Continue until all
the rice mixture is used.

Line the bottom of a heavy saucepan with a layer of unfilled cabbage
leaves and place the filled triangles on top. Cover with the remaining
oil, and add water as needed. Weigh down the cabbage with a heavy
plate, and with the pot covered, simmer slowly for about 30 minutes.
Carefully remove the dolmádes from the pot with a slotted spoon. Serve
hot or at room temperature.

Serves 6

ASSEMBLING THE DOLMADES

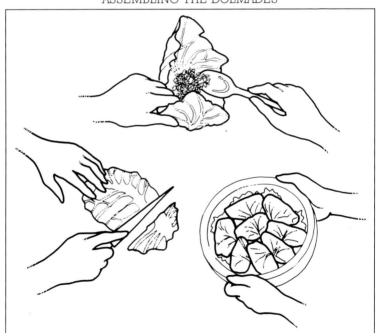

1. After parboiling, cut the cabbage into 2 cm (1 in) strips. **2.** Put a tbsp of
filling at one end of the strip and fold over into a triangle. **3.** Line the bottom of
the pot with leaves and fill with dolmádes. **4.** Press down with a heavy plate.

Stuffed Grape Leaves

Ντολμάδες Γιαλαντζί

Dolmádes yialanjí, as they are called in Greece, are exported in tins, and are widely available in Greek groceries in Europe and America. The homemade variety keeps well in the refrigerator, and is infinitely more subtle in its delicate flavor. Use tender grape leaves and fresh herbs for best results. You may blanch and freeze fresh grape leaves to have them available all year.

70 grape leaves, fresh, bottled or tinned
6 grated onions, or 15 finely chopped green onions
12 cl (½ cup) olive oil
400 g (2 cups) rice
15 g (6 tbsp) finely chopped dill, parsley or mint
2 tbsp pine nuts
Salt and freshly ground black pepper
2 lemons, juice only
50 to 75 cl (2 to 3 cups) water
Lemon slices for garnish

If using fresh grape leaves, blanch them first. If using bottled or tinned leaves, wash thoroughly to remove salt. Gently sauté the onions in 4 tbsp of olive oil, then stir in the rice and sauté a few minutes more. Add the dill and pine nuts and season with salt and pepper.
Put a teaspoon of rice mixture on the nonshiny surface of each grape leaf. Fold the sides inward and roll up loosely.
Line the bottom of a saucepan with a layer of unfilled grape leaves. Arrange the stuffed grape leaves in layers on top. Add the lemon juice, the remaining olive oil, salt and pepper, and enough water to cover.
Weigh down the stuffed grape leaves with a plate, cover the saucepan, and simmer for 40 to 45 minutes, until the liquid is absorbed and the rice is cooked. Add more water if necessary to prevent sticking.
Cool the stuffed grape leaves uncovered in the saucepan. Carefully transfer them to a serving dish and garnish with slices of lemon. Serve with thick plain yogurt for a mezé.
Makes about 60 stuffed grape leaves

Dolmádes Avgolémono

Ντολμάδες Αυγολέμονο

Dolmádes are sometimes served with plain yogurt instead of avgolémono sauce. They may be made with blanched cabbage or lettuce leaves, trimmed of any thick stalks. I have heard that even tender mulberry leaves may be used! Dolmádes are the basis of a light meal, accompanied by french fried potatoes and a salad, or they make an excellent first course.

40 to 50 fresh grape leaves, blanched (or tinned or bottled leaves, very well washed)

Stuffing
500 g (1 lb) ground beef, veal, pork, or a mixture
6 green onions, finely chopped
3 tbsp finely chopped parsley
1 tbsp finely chopped mint or dill
3 tbsp short grain rice
2 tbsp olive oil
6 cl (¼ cup) water
Salt and freshly ground black pepper

Cooking liquid
¾ liter (3 cups) beef or veal stock (or 2 bouillon cubes dissolved in ¾ liter hot water)
30 g (2 tbsp) butter
Salt and pepper

Avgolémono sauce
30 g (2 tbsp) butter
1 tbsp flour
2 lemons, juice only
2 eggs, well beaten
Salt and freshly ground black pepper

Combine all the stuffing ingredients and mix well.

To assemble the dolmádes, place a teaspoon of the stuffing on the non-shiny surface of each grape leaf. Fold the sides of leaf inward and roll up loosely. Line a saucepan with unfilled grape leaves and arrange the dolmádes in layers on top. Cover them with any remaining unfilled grape leaves. Add the stock, the butter, and salt and pepper. Weigh the dolmádes down with a plate, cover the saucepan, and simmer for one hour. Pour off the cooking liquid into a bowl and reserve.

Next, prepare the avgolémono sauce. In a small saucepan, melt 2 tbsp butter, add the flour, and cook and stir over low heat for two minutes. Slowly add the cooking liquid from the dolmádes, stirring constantly with a wire whisk. Add the lemon juice. Cook and stir until the sauce boils and thickens, about 5 to 10 minutes. Remove the pan from the heat, quickly beat in the eggs and season with salt and pepper.

Either pour the sauce over the dolmádes or serve it in a separate bowl.

Serves 6 as a main course. Makes about 35 stuffed grape leaves

Eggplant Papoutsákia

Μελιτζάνες Παπουτσάκια

A difficult recipe, but well worth the effort. Papoutsákia means "little shoes", which the stuffed eggplant halves resemble. This is a very rich dish, and one half eggplant per person is usually sufficient. You may omit the béchamel sauce if time or your diet dictates.

4 short fat eggplant, cut in half lengthwise
500 g (1 lb) ground beef or veal
¼ liter (1 cup) olive oil for sautéing
Salt and freshly ground black pepper
1 medium-sized onion, finely chopped
2 tbsp butter or olive oil
¼ liter (1 cup) dry white wine
3 medium-sized tomatoes, halved, seeded and grated,
skins discarded
25 g (½ cup) finely chopped parsley
Cinnamon and nutmeg
¼ tsp sugar
Salt and freshly ground black pepper
100 g (1 cup) breadcrumbs
2 egg whites
Béchamel sauce
60 g (2 oz) butter
30 g (¼ cup) flour
½ liter (2 cups) milk
2 egg yolks
Salt and freshly ground black pepper
Nutmeg
100 g (3/4 cup) grated kephalotýri or Parmesan cheese

Heat about 2 cm (1 in) of olive oil in a large frying pan and sauté the eggplant halves on each side until tender. (Alternatively, bake the eggplant halves in a moderate oven for 30 minutes, or until tender). Arrange the eggplant close together in an oiled baking dish, cut side up. Mash the flesh down with a fork. Sprinkle with salt and pepper.

To prepare the stuffing, sauté the onion in 2 tbsp butter or olive oil until transparent. Add the meat and simmer for 15 minutes. Add the wine, tomatoes and parsley, and season with the cinnamon, nutmeg, sugar, salt and pepper. Cover the pan and simmer for 20 minutes until almost all the liquid has evaporated. Remove from the heat, add 2 tbsp of breadcrumbs and the egg whites; mix well. Use the mixture to stuff the eggplant halves.

Make a thick béchamel sauce with the butter, flour and milk; cool it slightly before beating in the egg yolks. Season to taste with salt, pepper, nutmeg and ⅔ of the cheese. Top each eggplant with several tablespoons of béchamel sauce, and sprinkle with the remaining grated cheese and breadcrumbs.

Bake in an oven preheated to 190°C (375°F) for 40 minutes, or until the papoutsákia are lightly browned.

Serves 8

Eggplant Stuffed with Cheese

Μελιτζάνες Γεμιστές με Τυρί

A lighter and modern version of imám baildí.

6 long eggplant of approximately equal length, stems removed
250 g (8 oz) kephalotýri or pecorino cheese, cut into 6 sticks
of equal size
¼ liter (1 cup) olive oil for sautéing
3 large tomatoes, halved, seeded and grated, skins discarded
¼ liter (1 cup) tomato juice
½ tsp sugar
Salt and freshly ground black pepper
12 cl (½ cup) dry white wine
1 tbsp finely chopped fresh basil

Make three lengthwise incisions in each eggplant. In a heavy frying pan, heat 1 cm (½ in) of olive oil and sauté the eggplant very gently until they are soft, turning them occasionally.

Meanwhile, prepare a tomato sauce in another saucepan. Simmer together the tomatoes, tomato juice, sugar, salt and pepper for 25 minutes, or until they thicken.

When the eggplant have softened, remove from the frying pan and pour off all but 1 tbsp of oil. Add the wine, basil and tomato sauce. Simmer for five minutes.

Remove any large seeds from the eggplant and stuff each one with a stick of cheese. Put the eggplant side by side in the tomato sauce and simmer, covered, for 30 minutes.

Serves 4 to 6

Stuffed Tomatoes

Ντομάτες Γεμιστές με Κιμά

12 large tomatoes
500 g (1 lb) ground beef or veal
1 medium-sized onion, grated, boiled in water for 5 minutes,
and drained
30 g (2 tbsp) butter
Salt and freshly ground black pepper
½ tsp sugar
3 medium-sized tomatoes, halved, seeded and grated,
skins discarded
100 g (½ cup) short grain rice
4 tbsp finely chopped parsley
3 tbsp olive oil
3 tbsp breadcrumbs

Cut the tops off the tomatoes and reserve them. Scoop out the flesh and sprinkle the insides with salt and pepper. Purée the flesh in a food mill or blender. Sauté the meat and onion in the butter; season with salt, pepper and sugar. When the liquid has evaporated, add the grated and the puréed tomatoes and simmer for 15 minutes. Stir in the rice and parsley. Stuff the tomatoes with this mixture.

Replace the tops and arrange the tomatoes in a baking dish just large enough to hold them. Pour over the oil; sprinkle with salt, pepper and breadcrumbs. Bake in an oven preheated to 190°C (375°F) for 1½ hours. *Variation:* Use this filling to stuff zucchini, eggplant or green peppers, but prick them well first.

Serves 4 to 6

Stuffed Tomatoes Santorini

Ντομάτες Γεμιστές με Μελιτζάνα

10 large tomatoes
500 g (1 lb) eggplant, peeled and coarsely grated
100 g (½ cup) rice
1 medium-sized onion, finely chopped
2 garlic cloves, finely chopped
30 g (2 tbsp) butter
2 tbsp pine nuts
2 tbsp currants
Salt and freshly ground black pepper
½ tsp sugar

Cut a slice off the top of each tomato and scoop out the flesh. Sprinkle the insides with a little salt and leave upside down to drain. Chop half the flesh into small pieces and purée the rest in a food mill or processor. Sauté the onion and garlic lightly in the butter until transparent. Add the eggplant and sauté 15 minutes more. Add the rice, chopped tomato, tomato purée, pine nuts and currants; season with salt, pepper and sugar. Simmer five minutes.

Stuff the tomatoes with the mixture and replace their tops. Arrange the stuffed tomatoes in a baking dish just large enough to hold them. Bake in an oven preheated to 190°C (375°F) for about 1½ hours, or until the tomatoes are tender and the rice is cooked.

Serves 6 to 8

Stuffed Tomatoes Zakynthos

Ζακυνθινές Γεμιστές Ντομάτες

These are tasty hot, lukewarm or cold. You might also try stuffing green peppers, fat zucchini and small plump eggplant with the same mixture, adding more tomato juice or pulp. Very often, the Zantiotes, from the Ionian island of Zakynthos, pop a few very large okra in the baking dish along with the potatoes.

12 large tomatoes, ripe but fairly firm
6 medium-sized tomatoes, halved, seeded and grated,
skins discarded
2 large onions, very finely chopped or grated
12 cl (½ cup) water
¼ liter (1 cup) olive oil
150 g (12 tbsp) short grain rice
4 tbsp finely chopped parsley
2 tbsp finely chopped mint
1 tbsp oregano
3 garlic cloves, finely chopped
Salt and freshly ground black pepper
2 tsp sugar
60 g (½ cup) pecorino, kephalotýri or Zakynthos ladotýri cheese,
cut in small pieces
3 medium-sized potatoes, cut in quarters or eighths

Slice the bottoms off each of the 12 tomatoes and reserve. Scoop out the inside flesh from the tomatoes, purée it in a food mill or processor, and combine with the grated tomatoes; set aside.

In a large frying pan, simmer the onions with the water for 10 minutes, or until transparent. Add half the olive oil and sauté 5 minutes more. Add the rice, herbs, garlic and half of the tomato mixture. Season with salt, pepper and sugar, and simmer the mixture for another 10 minutes. Stir in the cheese.

Stuff the tomatoes with the rice mixture and replace the bottom slices. Put the tomatoes side by side in a baking dish just large enough to hold them.

Add the remaining olive oil to the remaining tomato mixture, season with salt, pepper and sugar, and pour the mixture over the stuffed tomatoes. Arrange the potatoes among the tomatoes.

Bake in a moderate oven preheated to 190°C (375°F), for 1½ hours, or until the tomatoes are tender. Add a little hot water if the bottom of the baking dish becomes dry. This dish may be served hot or at room temperature.

Serves 6 to 8

Tomatoes Stuffed
with Eggplant and Peppers

Ντομάτες Γεμιστές με Μελιτζάνες και Πιπεριές

*This delicious and succulent dish is marvelous as a first course, or for a buffet
luncheon or dinner.*

8 large tomatoes
100 g (½ cup) short grain rice
1 medium-sized eggplant, unpeeled and grated
1 medium-sized onion, finely chopped
60 gr (4 tbsp) butter
2 green peppers, finely chopped
Salt and freshly ground black pepper
½ tsp sugar
4 tbsp grated kephalotýri, pecorino or Parmesan cheese
2 eggs, beaten
4 tbsp finely chopped parsley
12 cl (½ cup) olive oil
2 tbsp breadcrumbs
3 potatoes, cut in eighths

Slice off the tops of each of the 8 tomatoes and reserve. Scoop out the
flesh from the tomatoes, chop it roughly and set aside. Sprinkle the interior of the shells with salt and leave upside down to drain.

In a large frying pan, sauté the onion in the butter until transparent. Add
the green pepper and eggplant; cook five to eight minutes. Add the rice
and half of the tomato flesh, and simmer for 10 minutes more. Season
with salt, pepper and ¼ tsp sugar, and cool slightly before stirring in
the cheese, eggs and parsley.

Stuff the tomatoes with this mixture and replace the tops. Transfer the
tomatoes to a baking dish just large enough to hold them. Purée the
remaining tomato flesh, mix it with the olive oil, and season with salt,
pepper and ¼ tsp sugar. Pour this over the tomatoes and sprinkle them
with breadcrumbs.

Fit in the potatoes among the tomatoes and season them with salt and
pepper. Bake in a moderate oven preheated to 190°C (375°F) for 1½
hours, or until the tomatoes are tender.

Serves 8

Stuffed Zucchini Avgolémono

Γεμιστά Κολοκυθάκια Αυγολέμονο

A summertime favorite.

12 fat zucchini, 10 cm (4 in) long, lightly scraped
500 g (1 lb) ground beef or veal
1 small onion, grated, parboiled 5 minutes, and drained
3 tbsp finely chopped parsley
2 tbsp olive oil
2 lemons, juice only
100 g (½ cup) short grain rice
Salt and freshly ground black pepper
Nutmeg
½ liter (2 cups) water
50 g (3 tbsp) butter
2 eggs, well beaten
¼ liter (1 cup) cream, optional

Cut off the stem end and hollow out the zucchini with a grapefruit spoon, melon baller, or potato peeler. Chop the flesh.

In a bowl, combine the meat, onion, parsley, olive oil, half of the lemon juice, the rice and 4 tbsp of the chopped zucchini flesh. Season with salt, pepper and nutmeg.

Stuff the zucchini with the mixture. Arrange them side by side in a saucepan. Add the water and 30 g (2 tbsp) of the butter. Simmer for 30 minutes. Add the remaining lemon juice to the beaten eggs. Slowly beat the zucchini cooking liquid into the egg mixture. Beat in the cream, if used.

Pour the sauce over the zucchini while shaking the saucepan.

If necessary, reheat very slowly without covering or boiling. Serve immediately.

Serves 6

Stuffed Zucchini Flowers

Γεμιστές Κολοκυθοκορφάδες

An exotic dish and a wonderful way to use zucchini flowers if you grow them in your garden.

18-24 zucchini flowers with the yellow pistil and stamens removed
400 g (2 cups) rice
1 medium-sized onion, finely chopped
80 cl (3½ cups) water
6 tbsp olive oil
2 tbsp finely chopped parsley
1 tbsp finely chopped mint
Salt and freshly ground black pepper

Boil the onion in 12 cl (½ cup) water for five minutes, or until soft. Add 3 tbsp of olive oil and sauté lightly for five minutes. Stir in ¼ liter (1 cup) of water, the parsley and the mint, and simmer for five minutes. Remove from the heat and add the rice, salt and pepper. Cover and set aside for five minutes so that the rice begins to swell.

Stuff each flower with the rice mixture and fold the petals over to close the opening. Place the stuffed flowers side by side in a shallow saucepan. Pour in ½ liter (2 cups) of water and the remaining olive oil; sprinkle with salt and pepper. Weigh the zucchini flowers down with a plate and simmer, covered, for 40 minutes.

Variation: Serve with an avgolémono sauce made from the cooking liquid as in the preceeding recipe. Or you may simmer the zucchini in tomato juice rather than water, for a completely different flavor.

Serves 6

Fish &
Shellfish

Athenian Boiled Fish

Ψάρι Βραστό

This dish can also be prepared in a different way. When the fish has cooked and cooled, remove it from the court-bouillon. Leaving the head and tail intact, remove all flesh from the bones. Chop the potatoes, carrots and zucchini into 1 cm (½ in) cubes. Using the best quality of mayonnaise available (and homemade is of course the first choice), combine the cubed vegetables with the fish into a salad. On a large oval dish, position the fish's head and tail in their proper place. Mound the fish salad to approximate the fish's body, and spread a layer of mayonnaise over to conceal the salad, leaving head and tail exposed. Now decorate the fish as your imagination fancies. Use capers, gherkins, lemon slices, beets, carrots, parsley, eggs and olives to create a buffet dish as lovely to look at as it is to eat, and call it Athinaikí Mayonaíza.

1 to 1½ kg (2 to 3 lb) whole white fish (red snapper, bass, grey mullet or hake)
Salt
Court-bouillon
4 carrots, peeled and cut in lengthwise quarters
4 zucchini, cut in 1 cm (½ in) slices
3 or 4 celery sticks, cut in 2 cm (1 in) pieces
2 or 3 medium-sized onions
12 small potatoes, peeled
1 large tomato (optional)
1 green pepper (optional)
2 bay leaves
Parsley sprigs
3 tbsp olive oil
4 tbsp lemon juice
½ tsp black peppercorns
2 liters (8 cups) water

Clean the fish by removing the scales, gills and other organs. Rinse well in cold water; sprinkle liberally with salt, and set aside.

To make the court-bouillon, use a stainless steel or enamelled saucepan that is large enough to hold the fish. Simmer all the ingredients except the potatoes and half of the lemon juice for 30 minutes, covered. Add the potatoes and continue simmering until they are just tender, about 20 minutes more. Strain the vegetables, reserve them and transfer the court-bouillon to a bowl. Wash the saucepan.

Return the court-bouillon to the pan and bring it to the boil with the remaining 2 tbsp lemon juice. Add the fish and simmer gently with the pan half-covered until the fish is just tender, about 15 minutes. Let the fish cool in the court-bouillon.

Carefully transfer the fish to a large platter and surround it attractively with the boiled vegetables. Garnish with parsley springs and capers. Serve the fish with homemade mayonnaise (see inside cover) or skordaliá (page 17), and plenty of lemon wedges. You may use the court-bouillon to prepare a fish avgolémono soup, page 32.

Serves 4 to 6

Fish and Eggplant au Gratin

Ψάρι με Μελιτζάνες ω Γκρατέν

500 g (1 lb) fillets of white fish (plaice, cod, sole or haddock)
1.5 kg (3 lb) eggplant, peeled and sliced 1 cm (½ in) thick
1 lit (1 qt) milk, or more
2 bay leaves
1 lemon, juice only
25 cl (1 cup) white wine
Salt and freshly ground black pepper
Cayenne pepper to taste
30 g (4 tbsp) grated Parmesan or Gruyère cheese
2 tbsp breadcrumbs
Margarine or butter for sautéing
50 g (3 tbsp) butter
3 tbsp flour

Sprinkle the eggplant liberally with salt and leave for 30 minutes.
Meanwhile, put the milk, bay leaves, salt and pepper in a saucepan that
is just large enough to hold the fish. Add the fillets and gently poach
them until soft. Strain the fish, reserving the liquid.
Wash and dry the eggplant. Melt about 2 cm (1 inch) of margarine or
butter in a frying pan and gently sauté the eggplant; don't brown it too
much. Drain on paper towels.
Butter a gratin dish and cover with a layer of eggplant. Arrange the fish
fillets on top.
Melt 3 tbsp of butter in a saucepan, add the flour and combine well.
Stirring constantly, add the fish liquid and cook until it has thickened. If
it becomes too thick, add a little more milk. Remove from the heat, stir in
the lemon juice, wine, salt and pepper. Pour the sauce over the fish,
sprinkle with the cheese, breadcrumbs and cayenne pepper. Dot with a
little additional butter and bake in an oven preheated to 170°C (350°F)
for about 25 minutes, until golden brown.
Serves 6

Naki's Fish Dish

Ψάρι της Νάκις

1 kg (2 lb) bream, bass, red snapper, or other white fish fillets,
sliced 3 cm (1 in) wide
½ tsp salt
1 lemon, juice only
3 medium-sized onions, sliced
2 medium-sized carrots, sliced
1 large potato, sliced
3 fresh tomatoes, skinned, seeded and coarsely chopped,
or one 380 g (12 oz) can of tomatoes
25 g (½ cup) finely chopped parsley
½ tsp black peppercorns
¼ liter (1 cup) olive oil
12 cl (½ cup) white wine

Rub the fish with the salt and lemon and set aside. Put the remaining
ingredients in a large shallow saucepan, heat, and simmer half-covered
for 45 minutes, or until the vegetables are tender. Add the fish and simmer for 15 minutes more, until the fish is just done. Serve hot.
Serves 4 to 6

Salt Cod Croquettes

Κροκέτες Μπακαλιάρου

500 g (2 cups) boiled salt cod, soaked, boned, skinned and
cut into small pieces
6 medium-sized potatoes, peeled, boiled and mashed
50 g (3 tbsp) butter, melted
2 or 3 eggs, lightly beaten
2 tbsp finely chopped onion
2 tbsp finely chopped parsley
Salt and freshly ground black pepper
¼ liter (1 cup) olive oil for sautéing

Combine all the ingredients. Shape into walnut-size balls or croquettes
and sauté slowly in the oil until golden brown. Drain on paper towels
and serve hot.

Serves 6 to 8

Fried Salt Cod

Τηγανητός Μπακαλιάρος

*Bakaliáros or salt cod, enjoys immense popularity in Greece. Greeks love
fish, and before freezing techniques were perfected, salting fish was the best
method of preserving it. Fried salt cod is served on March 25, Greece's Inde-
pendence Day, and Palm Sunday. It's best served piping hot.*

1 kg (2 lb) salt cod
Batter
150 g (1 cup) flour
1 tsp baking powder
2 eggs, separated
12 cl (½ cup) milk
1 tbsp olive oil
1 tbsp lemon juice
Nutmeg
Salt and freshly ground black pepper
Olive or corn oil for deep-frying

Soak the salt cod in cold water for 24 hours, changing the water several
times.
Prepare the batter by sifting the flour and baking powder together. Add
the egg yolks, mix well, then stir in the milk, olive oil and lemon juice.
Season with salt, pepper and nutmeg. Beat the egg whites until stiff and
fold them into the mixture to make a thick batter.
Prepare skordaliá, following the recipe on page 17.
Cut the fish into serving portions and remove the skin and bones. Dip
the fish into the batter and deep-fry in hot olive or corn oil until golden
brown. Drain on paper towels and serve hot with a bowl of skordaliá.

Serves 6

Red Mullet Marinata

Μπαρμπούνια Μαρινάτα

Fish cooked in this way will keep for several days. You may use almost any kind of fish, including the less expensive mackerel or sardine, and the piquant sauce will improve the flavor.

1 kg (2 lb) small red mullet, cleaned and scaled
125 g (1 cup) flour
¼ liter (1 cup) olive oil
1 tbsp dried rosemary
¼ liter (1 cup) vinegar
¼ liter (1 cup) water
1 tbsp finely chopped parsley
1 bay leaf
2 garlic cloves, finely chopped
Salt and freshly ground black pepper

Dredge the red mullet in the flour. Heat the olive oil in a frying pan and working in batches, sauté the fish slowly for about five minutes on each side. Drain on paper towels. Reserve the olive oil in a bowl and clean the frying pan.

Return the oil to the pan and stir in 2 tablespoons of flour and the rosemary. Cook and stir until the flour browns. Add the vinegar, water, parsley, bay leaf, garlic, salt and pepper. Simmer for 10 minutes. Transfer the fish to a serving dish and pour the sauce over the top. Serve hot.

Serves 4 to 6

Baked Sardines

Σαρδέλες στον Φούρνο

An excellent dish for true fish lovers.

1 kg (2 lb) fresh sardines, cleaned, heads removed, and boned
¼ liter (1 cup) olive oil
1 lemon, juice only
½ liter (2 cups) tomato juice
Salt and freshly ground black pepper
1 tbsp chopped fresh basil

Arrange the sardines side by side in a baking dish. Pour over them the olive oil, lemon juice and tomato juice. Season with salt, pepper and the basil.
Bake in a moderate oven, preheated to 200°C (400°F) for 15 minutes. Let cool and serve at room temperature.
Serves 6

Octopus Vinaigrette

Χταπόδι Βραστό με Λαδόξιδο

Octopus is abundant in Greece. It's a real favorite grilled over charcoal and accompanied by ouzo. A common late afternoon sound is that of someone beating a freshly caught octopus on the rocks at the beach to tenderize the flesh. It takes about half an hour, but the job can be accomplished at home using a mallet, or by freezing a fresh octopus for at least one month. The beating (or freezing) is only necessary for large octopus, 10 cm (4 in) or more.

1 kg (2 lb) fresh or frozen octopus, cleaned
¼ liter (1 cup) red wine
4 tbsp (¼ cup) olive oil
2 tbsp vinegar
1 tsp oregano

Place the octopus in a saucepan without water. Cover and let it cook slowly in the juices which exude from it. If necessary, add a little water occasionally to prevent sticking. After about 30 minutes, or when the octopus is tender, add the wine and stir. Cook for five minutes more, uncovered. Remove the octopus from the saucepan and slice it into bite-sized pieces. Transfer to a serving dish, pour the oil and vinegar over and sprinkle with oregano.
Serves 6 to 8

PREPARING THE OCTOPUS

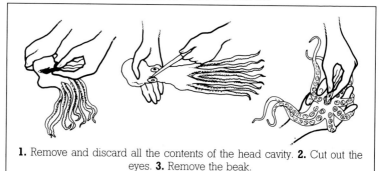

1. Remove and discard all the contents of the head cavity. **2.** Cut out the eyes. **3.** Remove the beak.

Octopus Crassato

Χταπόδι Κρασάτο

1 kg (2 lb) octopus, cleaned
12 cl (½ cup) olive oil
¼ liter (1 cup) dry white wine
150 g (1 cup) pitted black olives
Salt and freshly ground black pepper

Put the octopus in a saucepan without water, cover, and simmer slowly for about 25 minutes, or until tender. The octopus should exude enough juice itself to prevent sticking, but if necessary add a little water. Remove the octopus and cut it into bite-sized pieces.
Add the olive oil to the same saucepan, return the octopus to the pan and sauté gently for five minutes. Add the wine and olives; season with salt and pepper. Simmer for 10 minutes more, or until the sauce has thickened. Serve as a mezé.

Serves 8

Baked Octopus

Χταπόδι στον Φούρνο

1 kg (2 lb) fresh or frozen octopus, cleaned
4 medium-sized onions, cut in halves
3 large ripe tomatoes, sliced
¼ liter (1 cup) wine
12 cl (½ cup) olive oil
Freshly ground black pepper

Place the whole octopus in a baking dish together with the onions, tomatoes, wine and olive oil; season with pepper. Bake in a moderate oven preheated to 190°C (375°F) for about two hours, or until the octopus is tender.

Serves 6 to 8

Octopus Pilaf

Χταπόδι Πιλάφι

You may try adding rice or ditali, a short cut macaroni, to the octopus while it cooks. When the octopus begins to get tender, add 100 g (½ cup) rice or 100 g (1 cup) ditali, and 150 ml (⅔ cup) hot water to the pan. Cover and simmer until the rice or ditali is cooked.

1.5 kg (3 lb) octopus, cut in bite-sized pieces
4 green onions, finely chopped
12 cl (½ cup) white wine
3 medium-sized tomatoes, halved, seeded and grated,
skins discarded
¼ liter (1 cup) olive oil
3 tbsp finely chopped parsley
½ tsp sugar
Salt and freshly ground black pepper

Sauté the green onions in the olive oil, then add the octopus. Simmer for about 15 minutes. Add the wine, tomatoes and parsley, and season with sugar, salt and pepper. Simmer uncovered for 30 minutes or until the sauce thickens. Serve over boiled rice.

Variation: Substitute cuttlefish for octopus.

Serves 6

Shrimp Mikrolímano

Γαρίδες με Φέτα

For serving, divide the shrimps equally among individual au gratin dishes before broiling. One can get at his sauce and melted féta much easier than by reaching across the table, Greek style.

500 g (1 lb) large shrimps, peeled but heads and tails left on,
black intestines removed
6 medium-sized tomatoes, peeled, seeded and puréed with
2 tbsp olive oil
3 tbsp finely chopped parsley
3 garlic cloves, finely chopped
8 cl (⅓ cup) olive oil
250 g (8 oz) féta cheese, cut in 2 cm (1 in) chunks
30 g (2 tbsp) butter
Salt and freshly ground black pepper
Tabasco sauce (optional)

Simmer the puréed tomatoes for 20 to 25 minutes, until they become a thick sauce.

Transfer the sauce to a shallow ovenproof dish and on it arrange the shrimp. Sprinkle with the parsley, garlic and olive oil, and top with the féta. Dot with butter and season with lots of black pepper, a little salt, and the tabasco sauce.

Broil the dish for 10 minutes, until the féta melts and bubbles. Serve with plenty of fresh bread to dip into the delicious sauce.

Serves 4

Shrimp Kastelórizo

Γαρίδες με Πατάτες Ραγκού

For this ragoût, use size no. 3 shrimps, which will give you about 30 shrimps per 500 gr (1 lb).

500 g (1 lb) shrimps, peeled and washed, black intestines removed
1 medium-sized onion, grated
12 cl (½ cup) olive oil
3 medium-sized tomatoes, halved, seeded and grated,
skins discarded
4 medium-sized potatoes, peeled and cut in walnut-size pieces
2 tbsp finely chopped parsley
Salt and freshly ground black pepper
½ tsp sugar

Sauté the onion in the olive oil until transparent. Add the shrimp and sauté for a minute or two. Add the tomatoes, potatoes and parsley, and season with salt, pepper and sugar. Add a little water if necessary to prevent sticking. Simmer until the potatoes are done, about 20 minutes.

Serve with a green salad.

Serves 4

Fried Squid

Καλαμαράκια Τηγανητά

Fry the squid bodies and heads separately, as cooking times differ.

1 kg (2 lbs) fresh or frozen small squid
½ tsp salt
150 g (1 cup) flour
Olive or other oil for frying
1 lemon, cut in wedges

First clean the squid. Pull the heads from the bodies; they come off easily. Remove the ink sacs, viscera, transparent cartilage and beaks, and discard. Wash the squid well and drain in a colander.
Dredge the squid with salted flour. Heat about 2 cm (1 in) of oil in a frying pan until it smokes. Fry the squid in batches until crisp, then drain on absorbent paper. Avoid overcooking the squid, as they will become tough. Serve with lemon wedges and salad in season.
Serves 4 to 6

PREPARING THE SQUID

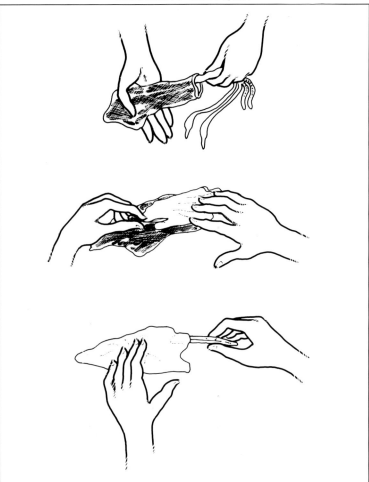

1. Remove the viscera and ink sac from the head. Pull the mucus membrane from the body. **2.** Gently pull the transparent cartilage away from the body.**3.** Squeeze the beak from the center of the tentacles. **4.** Ready to fry.

Stuffed Squid

Γεμιστά Καλαμάρια

This dish requires a little patience, but is magnificent. Small squid are the tastiest for stuffing and worth the additional effort. Serve with skordaliá, page 17, and beet or potato salad.

500 g (1 lb) fresh or frozen, small to medium-sized squid
2 green onions, chopped
12 cl (½ cup) olive oil
3 tbsp uncooked rice
3 tbsp finely chopped parsley
1 tbsp finely chopped dill
1 tbsp pine nuts
1 tbsp currants (optional)
200 g (6 oz) canned tomatoes, chopped
1 tbsp lemon juice
1 tbsp brandy
Salt and pepper
12 cl (½ cup) dry white wine

Wash and clean the squid. Remove the heads, tentacles, and triangular fins, and chop them finely. Reserve the bodies.

To prepare the stuffing, sauté the onions in half of the olive oil. Add the chopped squid and sauté a few minutes more. Add the rice, parsley, dill, pine nuts, currants, and half of the tomatoes. Sauté another few minutes, then add the lemon juice and brandy. Simmer until the liquid has evaporated. Season with salt and pepper.

Stuff the bodies of the squid about three-quarters full and sew up the openings with thread. Sauté the stuffed squids quickly on all sides in the remaining olive oil, then transfer them to a 18 by 24 cm (8 by 12 in) baking dish. Reserve the oil.

Pour the wine, the remaining tomatoes and the oil over the squid; season with salt and pepper. Bake in a moderate oven preheated to 190°C (375°F) for 30 minutes. Lower the oven temperature to 150°C (300°F), cover the baking dish with foil, and bake 30 minutes more. Remove the threads and serve.

Serves 4

STUFFING SQUID

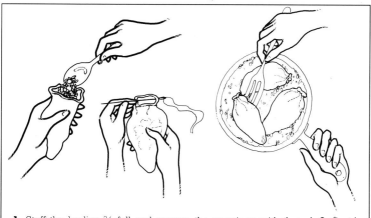

1. Stuff the bodies ¾ full and sew up the openings with thread. **2.** Sauté quickly on all sides in olive oil. **3.** Bake in a moderate oven, remove threads and serve.

Poultry

Chicken Avgolémono

Κοτόπουλο με Κρεμμύδια Αυγολέμονο

A fine marriage of flavors: chicken, onion, wine, lemon and eggs. This is a good choice for either a buffet or dinner menu.

1.5 kg (3 lb) chicken, cut into serving pieces, washed and dried
6 medium-sized onions, finely sliced
4 tbsp olive oil
¼ liter (1 cup) white wine
2 tbsp water
Salt and freshly ground black pepper
2 egg yolks
2 lemons, juice only
2 tbsp finely chopped parsley

Wash and dry the chicken.
Heat 2 tbsp of the olive oil in a large flameproof casserole and sauté the onions until transparent. Remove them and reserve.
Add the remaining oil and sauté the chicken pieces on all sides. Return the onions to the pan and add the wine, water, salt and pepper. Cover and simmer for 25 minutes or until the chicken is tender. Remove from the heat.
Beat the egg yolks well and add the lemon juice to them. Pour the mixture over the chicken, shake the pan and stir, but do not boil or cover the pan, as the sauce will curdle. Garnish with chopped parsley and serve with plain rice.
Serves 4 to 6

Chicken Arvanitiko

Αρβανίτικο Κοτόπουλο

This dish is especially popular among Greeks from the north.

1.5 kg (3 lb) chicken, cut into serving pieces
2 tbsp olive oil
3 medium-sized tomatoes, halved, seeded and grated, skins discarded
150 g (1 cup) blanched almonds, lightly roasted and coarsely ground
3 garlic cloves, finely chopped
1 sprig of rosemary
¼ liter (1 cup) dry red wine
½ tsp sugar
Salt and freshly ground black pepper

Wash and dry the chicken.
In a large flameproof casserole, sauté the chicken pieces in the olive oil until golden on all sides. Add the tomatoes, almonds, garlic, rosemary, wine and sugar; season with salt and pepper.
Cover and simmer for 30 minutes, or until the chicken is tender and the sauce thickens. If necessary, add a little hot water from time to time to prevent sticking. Serve with plain pilaf.
Serves 4 to 6

Broiled Lemon Chicken

Κοτόπουλο στη Σχάρα με Λεμόνι

The chicken will cook more evenly if you beat it with a wooden mallet before marinating.

1.5 kg (3 lb) chicken, cut into 8 serving pieces
3 lemons, juice only
12 cl (½ cup) olive oil
Salt and freshly ground black pepper
4 tsp oregano

Put the chicken in a bowl, pour over it the lemon juice and olive oil, and sprinkle liberally with salt, pepper and oregano. Mix well and let the chicken marinate for at least one hour.
Barbeque or broil the chicken for 10 minutes on each side. Serve with pilaf or mashed potatoes and a large salad.
Serves 4 to 6

Chicken Crassáto

Κοτόπουλο Κρασάτο

1.5 kg (3 lb) chicken, cut into 8 serving pieces
6 cl (¼ cup) olive oil
¼ liter (1 cup) dry white wine
1 sprig of rosemary
Salt and freshly ground black pepper

Wash and dry the chicken.
In a large shallow saucepan, heat the olive oil and sauté the chicken until lightly browned on all sides. Add the wine and sauté five minutes more. Add the rosemary, salt and pepper.
Cover and simmer for about 30 minutes or until the chicken is just tender. If the cooking liquid has evaporated, add some boiling water to the pan. This dish is delicious served with mashed potatoes and green salad.
Serves 4 to 6

Chicken Kokkinistó

Κοτόπουλο Κοκκινιστό

1.5 kg (3 lb) chicken, cut into serving pieces
4 tbsp (¼ cup) olive oil
1 large onion, grated
6 tomatoes, halved, seeded and grated, skins discarded
4 tbsp (¼ cup) finely chopped parsley
3 garlic cloves, finely chopped (optional)
Salt and freshly ground black pepper
½ tsp sugar

Wash and dry the chicken pieces. Sauté them in the olive oil until lightly browned. Add the onion and stirring constantly, sauté two to three minutes more. Then add the tomatoes, parsley and garlic. Season with salt, pepper and sugar.
Cover and simmer for 30 minutes or until the chicken is just tender. Serve with noodles or rice.
Serves 4 to 6

Chicken Sauté Zákynthos

Ζακυνθινό Χωριάτικο Κοτόπουλο

This is one dish that is better made with tomato paste, rather than fresh toma-toes. Surprisingly, the twenty cloves of garlic don't overpower the other flavors, and the garlic blends well with the cinnamon, cloves and bay leaves to make a spicy sauce.

1.5 kg (3 lb) chicken, cut into serving pieces, liver, heart
and gizzard chopped and reserved
3 tbsp olive oil
1 tbsp tomato paste
¼ liter (1 cup) water
20 garlic cloves, crushed
1 stick cinnamon
3 cloves
2 bay leaves
Salt and freshly ground black pepper
½ tsp sugar

Wash and dry the chicken. In a large covered frying pan, sauté the chopped liver, heart and gizzard lightly in the olive oil. Remove them from the pan and set aside. In the same oil and frying pan, sauté the chicken pieces until lightly browned.

Dilute the tomato paste in the water and add it to the chicken. Add the garlic, cinnamon, cloves, bay leaves and reserved giblets. Season with the salt, pepper and sugar.

Cover and simmer for about 30 minutes, or until the chicken is done and the sauce has thickened. Serve with brown bread and a salad.

Serves 4 to 6

Chicken with Orange

Κοτόπουλο με Πορτοκάλι

An excellent choice for a dinner party. This dish is unusual, easy to prepare, and magnificently tasty.

1.5 kg (3 lb) chicken, cut in serving pieces
4 oranges, juice strained
2 oranges, rind grated
2 tbsp butter
12 cl (½ cup) vermouth
12 cl (½ cup) brandy
Salt and white pepper
12 cl (½ cup) water

Wash and dry the chicken pieces.
In a flameproof casserole, heat the butter and sauté the chicken on all sides. Add the vermouth, brandy and orange juice; season with salt and pepper. Cover and simmer the chicken very slowly until just tender, about 20 minutes.

Meanwhile boil the orange rind in the water for 10 minutes; strain and add it to the chicken just before serving. Serve with plain rice and a green salad.

Serves 4 to 6

Chicken with Okra

Κοτόπουλο με Μπάμιες

This chicken and okra ragoût, seasoned with a rich tomato sauce, may be eaten cold if cooked with olive oil, but must be served hot if you use the butter. So that the okra doesn't lose its shape, trim the stem end carefully. Don't cut through to the interior chamber, but cut the tops in a conical shape.

1.5 kg (3 lb) chicken, cut in 8 serving pieces
1 kg (2 lb) okra, stalks removed and trimmed
1 medium-sized onion, finely chopped
12 cl (½ cup) butter or olive oil
3 tomatoes, halved, seeded and grated, skins discarded
2 tbsp finely chopped parsley
Salt and freshly ground black pepper
½ tsp sugar

Wash and dry the chicken pieces. Heat the butter (or oil) in a large saucepan. Sauté the chicken and onions together until the chicken is lightly browned on all sides. Next add the tomatoes, okra and parsley and season with salt, pepper and sugar.
Cover and simmer slowly for 30 minutes or until the chicken and okra are tender. Stir from time to time, and if necessary to prevent sticking, add a little hot water to the pan. Serve with fresh bread.

Serves 4 to 6

Boned Stuffed Chicken Marinos

Γεμιστό Κοτόπουλο χωρίς Κόκαλα

An excellent dish for a dinner party. Prepare it the day before needed, so that it can be sliced easily when cold, then reheated in its gravy. Make sure you tie the roll up carefully to keep the cheese from bubbling out during cooking.

1.5 kg (3 lb) chicken
1 onion
1 carrot
2 celery sticks
2 bay leaves
Salt and freshly ground black pepper
3 tbsp finely chopped parsley
1 tsp fresh rosemary leaves, finely chopped
2 tbsp grated féta, Gruyère, or Gouda cheese
4 slices streaky bacon
1 garlic clove, crushed
30 g (2 tbsp) butter
12 cl (½ cup) white wine

Working carefully, remove the skin from the chicken in one piece and reserve. Remove the flesh from the bones.

Make a stock by boiling the bones together with the onion, carrot, celery, bay leaves and salt in water to cover.

Spread the chicken skin on a flat surface and remove any large pieces of fat. Arrange half of the chicken flesh on the skin, and sprinkle it with the parsley, rosemary and cheese. Place the rest of the chicken on top; season with salt and pepper.

Fold the chicken skin over to form as neat a roll as possible. Wrap the bacon around the roll and tie it up with a string. Rub the roll with the garlic. Melt the butter in a large saucepan and sauté the chicken roll on all sides. Add the wine and 1 cup of the stock. Cover the saucepan and simmer very slowly until done, about 1 hour. Let the chicken roll cool before slicing it, then reheat the slices in its gravy.

Serve the chicken roll with spinach purée and French fried potatoes. Save the leftover stock to use as a base for avgolémono soup (page 32).

Serves 6

TO BONE AND STUFF A CHICKEN

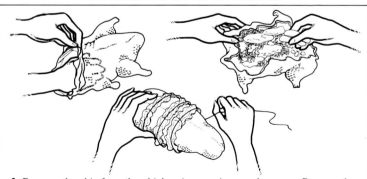

1. Remove the skin from the chicken in one piece and reserve. Remove the flesh. **2.** Spread the skin out on a flat surface. Arrange half of the chicken flesh on the skin. Add parsley, rosemary and cheese, and place remaining chicken on top. **3.** Fold chicken skin over to form a neat roll. Wrap with bacon and tie up with string.

Chicken Croquettes

Κροκέτες από Κοτόπουλο

350 g (3 cups) chopped cooked chicken
½ liter (2 cups) very thick
Béchamel sauce (see inside cover)
1 egg yolk
Salt and freshly ground black pepper
1 pinch nutmeg
100 g (1 cup) breadcrumbs
½ liter (2 cups) oil for deep-frying

Combine the chicken, béchamel sauce and egg yolk. Season the mixture with salt, pepper and nutmeg. Keeping your hands wet while you work, shape the mixture into 7 cm (3 in) croquettes.
Roll the croquettes in breadcrumbs and leave them in the refrigerator to dry for at least one hour.
Heat the oil and fry the croquettes in batches until golden brown. Drain the croquettes well on paper towels and serve with tomato sauce, page 40.

Serves 6

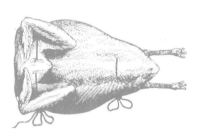

Roast Chicken and Potatoes

Κοτόπουλο και Πατάτες στον Φούρνο

A simple classic of Greek cuisine. If you parboil the potatoes for five minutes before baking them, the inside becomes more soft and flaky and the outside even more crispy. First prepare the chicken and get it in the oven, then parboil the potatoes and add them to the baking dish, stirring so they are coated with the oil and drippings. Parboiled, they only need to roast for an hour.

1.5 kg (3 lb) chicken
6 to 8 potatoes, peeled and cut in lengthwise quarters
2 lemons, juice only
2 tbsp olive oil
Salt and freshly ground black pepper
Oregano

Place the chicken in a baking dish and surround it with the potatoes. The dish should be just large enough to hold everything. Pour the lemon juice and olive oil over all and season well with salt, pepper and oregano. Bake in an oven preheated to 200°C (400°F) for about 1½ hours, basting occasionally.

Serves 4 to 6

Roast Stuffed Chicken

Γεμιστό Κοτόπουλο στον Φούρνο

1.5 kg (3 lb) chicken, liver, heart and gizzard
finely chopped and reserved
6 to 8 potatoes, peeled and cut in lengthwise quarters
6 tbsp olive oil
12 cl (½ cup) dry wine or light sherry
200 g (2 cups) breadcrumbs
60 g (½ cup) grated Zakynthos ladotýri, Parmesan or
pecorino cheese
2 garlic cloves, finely chopped
2 tsp oregano
2 lemons, juice only
1 egg, beaten
Salt and freshly ground black pepper
1 bay leaf

To prepare the stuffing, sauté the chopped liver, heart and gizzard in 2 tbsp of olive oil. Add the wine, boil for three to four minutes, then add the breadcrumbs, cheese, garlic, oregano and 1 tbsp of lemon juice. Stir well and simmer for five minutes. Cool the mixture slightly and stir in the beaten egg; season with salt and pepper.

Wash the chicken and dry it well inside and out; sprinkle with salt and pepper and place the bay leaf inside. Fill the chicken with the stuffing and sew it up. Put the chicken in a roasting pan, surround it with the potatoes, and sprinkle with salt and pepper. Pour over the remaining olive oil and lemon juice. Roast in an oven preheated to 190°C (375°F) for about two hours, basting occasionally.

Serves 4 to 6

Chicken with Bulgur Soufli

Κοτόπουλο με Πλιγούρι

1.5 (3 lb) chicken, cut into 8 serving pieces
6 tbsp bulgur or pligoúri
¼ liter (1 cup) olive oil
1 tsp cinnamon
¼ tsp cayenne pepper
2 tomatoes, halved, seeded and grated, skins discarded
4 tbsp (¼ cup) water
Salt and pepper
½ tsp oregano

Wash and dry the chicken. Brown the chicken and spices in olive oil in a large casserole. Add the tomatoes, water, salt and pepper. Cover and cook for 25 minutes.

Remove the chicken from the pan. Add the bulgur and oregano, cover and simmer for 30 minutes. Return the chicken to the pan and continue cooking, covered, until all the liquid has been absorbed, about 10 minutes more.

Serves 4 to 6

Cold Chicken in Creamy Eggplant Sauce

Κρύο Κοτόπουλο με Σάλτσα Μελιτζάνας

A delightful dish for a hot summer day. The eggplant's smoky flavor makes the sauce most unusual. Use the remaining stock for an avgolémono soup.

1.5 kg (3 lb) chicken
Stock
2 onions
2 carrots
4 or 5 celery sticks
Several sprigs of parsley
2 bay leaves
1 lemon, juice strained
Salt and freshly ground black pepper
Sauce
1 medium-sized eggplant
1 tbsp butter
1 tbsp flour
2 tbsp lemon juice
½ tsp grated lemon rind
12 cl (½ cup) fresh cream
2 tsp Dijon mustard
1 green pepper, finely chopped
3 tbsp finely chopped parsley
1 tomato, thinly sliced

To prepare the chicken, put it in a large pot and barely cover it with water. Add the onions, carrots, celery, sprigs of parsley, bay leaves, lemon juice and salt. Bring to the boil and simmer for 45 minutes, or until the chicken is just done. Let cool for 20 minutes in the stock.

Meanwhile, broil the eggplant over direct heat for 20 minutes, until soft. Cool slightly. Carefully scoop out the flesh, discard the seeds, and mash it well.

To prepare the sauce, melt the butter in a saucepan. Add the flour, cook and stir for one to two minutes, then slowly add ¼ liter (1 cup) of the chicken stock, stirring until it boils. Remove from the heat and let it cool. Add the lemon juice and rind, the cream and mashed eggplant. Season well with salt, pepper and Dijon mustard.

Remove the bones and skin from the chicken and arrange the meat attractively on a serving dish. Cover it with the eggplant sauce, sprinkle with chopped green pepper and parsley, and surround with the tomato slices.

Serves 6

Meat

Moussaká

Μουσακάς με Μελιτζάνες

Moussaká is virtually the national dish of Greece, and the one to which most foreigners are first introduced. The classic proportion is at least twice as much eggplant as ground meat. Make sure that the eggplant is fresh. In Greece ground beef is the meat of choice for this dish. To make the moussaká somewhat lighter, you may drain the fried eggplant in a colander overnight. Or some cooks fry only half of the eggplant, then brush the rest with olive oil and broil until tender. Either method will make the dish less rich, but in any case, moussaká is not a dish for dieters! In the course of preparation, you will use most of the pots in your kitchen; so allow plenty of time for preparation and clean up, and your efforts will be well rewarded.

1.5 kg (3 lb) eggplant, cut in slices 1 cm (½ in) thick
¼ liter (1 cup) olive oil for sautéing
Meat Sauce
500 g (1 lb) ground beef or veal
1 medium-sized onion, finely chopped
1 tbsp butter
¼ liter (1 cup) white wine
3 medium-sized tomatoes, halved, seeded and grated,
skins discarded
3 tbsp finely chopped parsley
½ tsp cinnamon (optional)
Salt and freshly ground black pepper
½ tsp sugar
¼ liter (1 cup) water
Béchamel Sauce
175 g (6 oz) butter
100 g (¾ cup) flour
1.5 liters (6 cups) milk
Salt and freshly ground black pepper
Nutmeg
2 eggs, beaten
125 g (1 cup) grated kephalotýri or Parmesan cheese
2 tbsp breadcrumbs

Salt the eggplant slices well and let them drain for 30 minutes in a colander. Sauté the onion in the butter until transparent. Add the meat; cook and stir constantly until it is crumbly. Add the remaining ingredients for the meat sauce and simmer uncovered until all the liquid is absorbed, about 20 minutes.

Meanwhile rinse and dry the eggplant slices. Heat 5 cm (2 in) of olive oil in a large frying pan and sauté the eggplant in batches, adding more olive oil as necessary. Be careful not to brown the eggplant too much, but fry until just golden. Drain well on paper towels or in a colander.

To prepare the béchamel sauce, melt all but 1 tbsp of the butter in a saucepan. Add the flour and cook and stir over low heat for 3 to 5 minutes. Add the milk slowly, stirring constantly with a wire whisk to avoid lumps. Continuing to stir, cook the sauce until it thickens and begins to boil. Season it with salt, pepper and nutmeg. Cool slightly, then beat in the eggs.

Now you are ready to assemble the moussaká. Arrange half of the eggplant slices in the bottom of a large baking dish. Spread with half of the meat sauce and sprinkle with a third of the grated cheese. Repeat the process. Pour the béchamel sauce evenly over all, then sprinkle with the breadcrumbs and the remaining third of the cheese.

Dot with the remaining tablespoon of butter.

Bake in an oven preheated to 190°C (375°F) until golden brown, about one hour. Cool for 20 minutes, then cut into squares.

Variation: Instead of fried eggplant, try substituting cooked artichoke hearts, or sautéed or steamed zucchini slices. Omit the tomatoes from the meat sauce.

Serves 8

Light Moussaká

Ελαφρύς Μουσακάς

By simmering the vegetables rather than frying them, you create a dish that is very light and delicious, and much lower in calories than traditional moussaká. The béchamel sauce is reduced in quantity.

1 kg (2 lb) large eggplant, peeled and cut in slices 1 cm (½ in) thick
500 g (1 lb) ground beef or veal
3 large potatoes, peeled and sliced
2 onions, finely sliced
4 tomatoes, peeled, seeded and sliced
12 cl (½ cup) beef stock (or 1 bouillon cube dissolved in 12 cl hot water)
3 tbsp olive oil
12 cl (½ cup) wine
½ liter (2 cups) tomato juice
2 tbsp finely chopped parsley
Salt and freshly ground black pepper
Béchamel Sauce
90 g (3 oz) butter
6 tbsp flour
¾ liter (3 cups) milk
1 egg, beaten
4 tbsp (¼ cup) grated kephalotýri or Parmesan cheese

Layer the eggplant, tomatoes, potatoes and onion in a large saucepan. Add the stock and 1 tbsp of olive oil. Cover and simmer about 20 minutes, or until the vegetables are tender.

In a large frying pan, heat 2 tbsp of olive oil and sauté the meat for five minutes. Add the wine, tomato juice and parsley, and simmer until all the liquid has evaporated. Season with salt and pepper.

Butter a 24 by 30 cm (9 by 12 in) baking dish and cover the bottom with the potatoes and onions. Add the meat sauce, the tomatoes, and lastly, the eggplant.

To prepare the béchamel sauce, melt the butter in a saucepan, add the flour and cook, stirring, for three to five minutes. Add the milk slowly while whisking constantly. Cook and stir until the sauce thickens and boils. Remove from the heat, cool slightly, then add the egg. Season with salt and pepper.

Pour the béchamel sauce over the eggplant and sprinkle with grated cheese. Cook in an oven preheated to 190°C (375°F), until the top is lightly browned, about 45 minutes.

Serves 6 to 8

Zákynthos Sáltsa

Ζακυνθινή Σάλτσα

This is the most popular dish on the Ionian island of Zákynthos. The addition of the pungent ladotýri, or its substitute pecorino, is what makes this dish unique.

1 kg (2 lb) stewing beef, cut into 2 cm (1 in) cubes
6 medium-sized tomatoes, halved, seeded and grated,
skins discarded
12 cl (½ cup) olive oil
4 garlic cloves, finely chopped
2 bay leaves
4 cloves (optional)
Salt and freshly ground black pepper
¼ tsp sugar
125 g (8 oz) kephalotýri, Zákynthos ladotýri or pecorino cheese,
cut in small cubes
2 tsp oregano

Dry the meat well. In a large flameproof casserole, heat the oil until it smokes. Add the meat and brown it quickly on all sides. Add the tomatoes, garlic, bay leaves and cloves; season with salt, pepper and sugar. Simmer covered for one hour, or until the meat is tender and the sauce thickens. If necessary, add a little hot water to prevent sticking. To further thicken the sauce, boil uncovered for several minutes at the end of cooking. Just before serving, stir in the cheese and oregano. Serve with mashed potatoes or boiled rice.

Serves 6

Veal with Leeks

Κρέας με Πράσα

Leeks are a popular vegetable in Greece, and their flavor combines well with that of the veal.

1 kg (2 lb) veal, cut in 2 cm (1 in) cubes
1.5 kg (3 lb) leeks, white parts only, cut in 7 cm (3 in) lengths
5 green onions, finely chopped
5 tbsp olive oil
3 medium-sized tomatoes, halved, seeded and grated,
skins discarded
Salt and freshly ground black pepper
½ tsp sugar
30 g (2 tbsp) butter
Croutons

In a flameproof casserole, sauté the green onions and meat together in the olive oil. Add the tomatoes and season with salt, pepper and sugar. Simmer until the meat is almost tender, about 45 minutes.
In another saucepan boil the leeks for 10 minutes. Drain well and add them to the meat. Simmer 15 minutes more, or until the leeks are tender. Stir in the butter and serve garnished with croutons.

Serves 6

Tas Kebáb

Τας Κεμπάμπ

This dish is often served on a small plate in tavérnas as a mezé.

1 kg (2 lb) stewing beef, cut in 2 cm (1 in) cubes
8 medium-sized onions, 4 finely chopped and 4 finely sliced
¼ liter (1 cup) water
1 tbsp fresh butter or olive oil
6 medium-sized tomatoes, halved, seeded and grated,
skins discarded
50 g (1 cup) finely chopped parsley
Salt and freshly ground black pepper
¼ tsp sugar

In a flameproof casserole, simmer the chopped onions in the water until
the liquid has evaporated and the onions are tender. Add the butter (or
olive oil), and sauté a few minutes more. Next, add the meat and the
sliced onions and sauté for five minutes. Then add the tomatoes and
parsley. Season with salt, pepper and the sugar.
Cover and cook very slowly until the meat is tender and the sauce has
thickened, about one hour. Serve with plain rice.
Variation: Add three or four sautéed sliced green peppers.
Serves 8

Ragoût of Meat and Green Beans

Κρέας με Φασόλια

*The combination of meat with one vegetable is classic fare in Greece. For best
results, choose a fresh, in-season vegetable.*

1 kg (2 lb) stewing beef or veal, or leg of lamb, cut into
serving pieces
1 kg (2 lb) green beans, fresh or frozen
2 medium-sized onions, chopped
3 tbsp olive oil
3 medium-sized tomatoes, peeled, seeded and chopped
4 tbsp (¼ cup) chopped parsley
Salt and freshly ground black pepper
½ tsp sugar

Sauté the meat and onions in the olive oil. Add the tomatoes and parsley; season with pepper and sugar. Cover and simmer for 30 minutes.
Add the green beans and simmer until the meat and beans are tender and the sauce has thickened, 30 to 45 minutes more. Add salt and
serve.
Variation: Substitute other vegetables for the green beans. Try fresh or
frozen peas, okra, thick slices of zucchini, chunks of eggplant, quartered potatoes, or a combination of several vegetables.
Serves 6 to 8

Beef Stifádo

Στιφάδο

Stifádo, with its hearty sweet-sour flavor, is a perfect cold weather meal. The standard proportion is to have twice as much onion as meat. Try to find small onions and soak them overnight to make them less overpowering and easier to digest.

1 kg (2 lb) stewing beef, cut in 2 cm (1 in) cubes
2 kg (4 lb) small onions, 2 cm (1 in) diameter
2 tbsp olive oil
30 g (2 tbsp) butter
3 medium-sized tomatoes, halved, seeded and grated,
skins discarded
3 garlic cloves, finely chopped
3 bay leaves
2 tbsp vinegar
Salt and freshly ground black pepper

On the day before you make this dish, peel the onions, cover them with cold water and leave them to soak overnight. The next day, discard the water and rinse the onions well.

In a large flameproof casserole, heat the olive oil and butter, and sauté the meat on all sides. Add the onions and the remaining ingredients; season with salt and pepper.

Add enough hot water to cover the stifado and simmer, covered, until the meat is tender and the gravy has thickened, about 1 hour. If the sauce needs more thickening, remove the lid and boil rapidly to reduce it. Serve with mashed potatoes and a salad.

Serves 6 to 8

Youvétsi

Γιουβέτσι

Youvétsi takes its name from the round deep earthenware dish in which it is baked. These dishes, traditionally made on the island of Siphnos, are glazed on the inside and unglazed outside. This beef, tomato and pasta stew is a great favorite of children.

1 kg (2 lb) stewing beef or lamb, cut into 6 serving pieces
500 g (1 lb) orzo, or other small cut macaroni
1 large onion, grated
3 tbsp butter or olive oil
Salt and freshly ground black pepper
¼ lit (1 cup) wine or sherry
6 medium-sized tomatoes, halved, seeded and grated,
skins discarded
½ tsp sugar
2 tbsp grated kephalotýri or Parmesan cheese

Preheat the oven to 190°C (375°F). In a round, deep baking dish, bake the onion in the olive oil (or butter), stirring occasionally until the onion becomes transparent. This technique gives the dish a special flavor. Now add the meat, season with salt and pepper, and roast for about one hour, or until the meat is nearly tender.

Add the wine and tomatoes; season with salt, pepper and sugar. Return the dish to the oven, and when the liquid comes to a boil, stir in the orzo. Bake for about 30 minutes, stirring occasionally. Add boiling water if needed to prevent sticking. The orzo should be neither overcooked nor too dry. Serve very hot with the grated cheese sprinkled on top.

Serves 6 to 8

Meat with Quinces

Κυδωνάτα

If you are lucky enough to find fresh quinces, this unusual dish makes wonderful use of them.

1.5 kg (3 lb) beef or pork, cut in 5 cm (2 in) cubes
1 kg (2 lb) quinces, cored and thickly sliced
1 medium-sized onion, finely chopped
125 g (½ cup) butter
3 medium-sized tomatoes, halved, seeded and grated,
skins discarded
Hot water
Salt and freshly ground black pepper
¼ tsp sugar

Dry the meat well. Heat the butter in a large flameproof casserole and sauté the meat and onion in it. Add the quinces and stir well. Add the tomatoes and enough hot water to cover. Season with salt, pepper and sugar.
Cover and simmer for one hour, or until the meat is tender and most of the liquid has evaporated.
Serves 8

Veal or Beef Pot Roast

Μοσχάρι Ψητό

As in the United States or Great Britain, pot roast is an old-time favorite for Sunday dinner.

1 to 1.5 kg (2 to 3 lb) topside, silverside or top rump of veal or beef
6 cl (¼ cup) olive oil
¼ liter (1 cup) dry red wine or dry sherry
1 sprig of rosemary
2 bay leaves
Salt and freshly ground black pepper

Have the roast tied by the butcher to preserve its shape. Dry the meat well. Heat the olive oil in a heavy flameproof casserole and brown the meat on all sides. Add the wine or sherry and boil rapidly for three to five minutes. Add the rosemary, bay leaves, salt and pepper.
Cover, reduce heat, and simmer slowly until tender, about two hours. Add a little boiling water occasionally if necessary to prevent sticking.
Serve with mashed potatoes, spaghetti or rice.
Serves 6 to 8

Sofríto

Σοφρίτο

Sofríto is the specialty of Corfu, and the most popular of the local dishes.

1 kg (2 lb) loin, shoulder or sirloin of veal, cut in 1 cm (½ in) slices
Seasoned flour
12 cl (½ cup) olive oil, or more
6 to 8 garlic cloves, finely chopped
¼ liter (1 cup) vinegar
3 tbsp finely chopped parsley
Salt and freshly ground black pepper
Hot water

Dredge the meat in the seasoned flour. Brown it in the olive oil and remove from the pan.
Discard all but 2 tbsp of olive oil. Gently sauté the garlic for one to two
minutes in the oil. Add the vinegar, bring to a boil, stir well and remove
from the heat.
Transfer the meat to a flameproof casserole. Pour over it the vinegar
mixture; season with the parsley, salt and pepper. Add enough hot water to just cover the meat. Partially cover the casserole and simmer for
about 45 minutes, or until the meat is tender and the sauce thickens.
Serve the sofríto with mashed potatoes and a salad.
Serves 6

Keftedákia

Κεφτεδάκια

*These small fried meatballs are wonderfully delicious as a main course or hot
mezé. Their soft texture is the result of using plenty of bread combined with the
ground beef. Keftedákia are practical finger food for a children's party, well-
received and easy to manage.*

500 g (1 lb) ground beef
6 to 8 slices day-old bread, crusts removed, soaked in water
and squeezed
1 small onion, finely chopped
25 g (½ cup) chopped parsley
1 garlic clove, finely chopped
3 tbsp grated Parmesan cheese
1 tbsp vinegar
1 tbsp ouzo (optional)
1 tbsp olive oil
1 tsp oregano
¼ tsp cinnamon
¼ tsp nutmeg
Salt and pepper
1 egg, slightly beaten
Flour
Oil for frying

Combine all the ingredients, adding enough cold water to make a fairly
stiff mixture. Knead well and shape into balls the size of a walnut. Roll
them in flour and fry in oil until well browned. Drain on paper towels and
serve hot with half a lemon on the side.
Serves 4. Makes about 25 keftedákia

Meatballs Avgolémono

Γιουβαρλάκια Αυγολέμονο

A delightful summer presentation for a year-round favorite.

Meatballs
500 g (1 lb) ground beef or veal
100 g (½ cup) rice
2 egg whites
3 green onions, finely chopped
3 tbsp water
2 tbsp olive oil
3 tbsp finely chopped parsley or dill
Salt and freshly ground black pepper
Sauce
¾ liter (3 cups) stock or water
2 egg yolks
1 lemon, juice only

Combine the meatball ingredients, reserving 1 tbsp of the parsley or dill. Knead well and form into walnut-size balls.

In a large saucepan, bring the water or stock to the boil and add the meatballs. Weigh them down with a plate; cover with a lid and simmer for 30 minutes.

In a small bowl, beat the egg yolks and add the lemon juice. Then beating constantly, add a few spoonfuls of the cooking liquid to the mixture. Slowly add the mixture to the meatballs while shaking the pan well. Season with salt and pepper, and sprinkle with the reserved parsley or dill. Serve with French fried potatoes.

Serves 4 to 6

Soutzoukákia

Σουτζουκάκια

The recipe for these spicy sausage shaped meatballs is from Smyrna in Asia Minor, present day Turkey.

Sausages
500 g (1 lb) ground beef
2 thick slices day-old bread, crusts removed, soaked in milk
and squeezed out
2 tsp ground cumin, or 1 tbsp lemon juice
1 garlic clove (or more), finely chopped
3 tbsp finely chopped parsley
1 egg, slightly beaten
Salt and freshly ground black pepper
Flour
Olive oil for sautéing
Sauce
3 medium-sized tomatoes, halved, seeded and grated,
skins discarded
15 g (1 tbsp) butter
1 bay leaf
½ tsp sugar

Combine the meat, bread, cumin (or lemon juice), garlic, parsley, egg, salt and pepper. Knead well. Form the mixture into small sausages about 5 cm (2 in) long. Roll in flour and sauté them on all sides in olive oil until browned.

To make the sauce, combine the tomatoes, butter, bay leaf, salt, pepper and sugar in a saucepan. Simmer for 30 minutes.

Place the browned sausages in the sauce and simmer for 15 minutes more. Serve with mashed potatoes or rice and yogurt.

Serves 4. Makes about 18 soutzoukákia

Meatballs Dodecanese

Ροδίτικοι Κεφτέδες

A variation on the keftedákia theme, these meatballs are flavored with plenty of onions, tomatoes, herbs and ouzo. This recipe is from the island of Rhodes.

1 kg (2 lb) ground beef
6 medium-sized onions, grated
3 medium-sized tomatoes, halved, seeded and grated,
skins discarded
50 g (1 cup) finely chopped parsley or mint
6 tbsp flour
6 cl (¼ cup) ouzo
2 tbsp lemon juice
Salt and freshly ground black pepper
Oil for deep-frying

Combine all the ingredients and knead well. The mixture should be rather soft. Shape into walnut-size balls, roll in some additional flour and deep-fry in batches until well browned. Serve immediately.

Serves 8

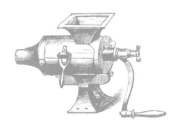

Biftékia

Μπιφτέκια

500 g (1 lb) ground beef
2 thick slices day-old bread, crusts removed, soaked in milk
and squeezed out
4 tbsp finely chopped parsley
2 tsp oregano
2 tbsp olive oil
1 tbsp Worcestershire sauce
Salt and freshly ground black pepper
Water as needed
Flour

Combine all the ingredients except the flour. Add a little water if necessary to make a fairly stiff mixture. Knead well.
Shape into 5 cm (2 in) patties, dip them in flour, and broil, fry or barbeque on both sides. Serve with lemon wedges and salad.

Serves 3 to 4

Beef and Zucchini Loaf

Κιμά Ρολό και Κολοκυθάκια

500 g (1 lb) ground beef or veal
500 g (1 lb) zucchini, grated and squeezed
2 thick slices day-old bread, crusts removed, soaked in milk
and squeezed out
3 green onions, finely chopped
30 g (¼ cup) grated Parmesan or kephalotýri cheese
2 tbsp olive oil
2 egg yolks
Salt and freshly ground black pepper

Combine all the ingredients and knead well. Shape into a loaf and
transfer to a shallow buttered roasting pan.
Bake in a moderate oven preheated to 190°C (375°F) for 1 hour. Serve
with tomato sauce, (page 40).
Serves 4 to 6

Meatballs in Tomato Sauce

Γιουβαρλάκια με Σάλτσα Ντομάτας

*Try stirring a few tablespoons of yogurt into the thickened sauce after
removing the cooked meatballs.*

500 g (1 lb) ground beef or veal
1 medium-sized onion, finely chopped
3 tbsp finely chopped parsley
100 g (½ cup) rice
1 egg, beaten
2 to 3 tbsp water
Salt and freshly ground black pepper
½ liter (2 cups) tomato juice
6 cl (¼ cup) olive oil
1 sprig of fresh basil
½ tsp sugar

Combine the meat, onion, parsley, rice, egg, water, salt and pepper.
Knead well. Shape the mixture into walnut-size balls.
In a saucepan, bring the tomato juice and oil to the boil. Season with
basil, salt, pepper and sugar. Add the meatballs one at a time. Simmer
for 25 minutes, until the meatballs are tender and the sauce thickens.
Serve with French fried potatoes or spaghetti.
Serves 6

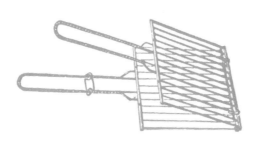

Leg of Lamb Riganáto

Αρνί Γεμιστό, με Ρίγανη

Several years ago we took a glorious trip down to the Peloponnese to a village near Sparti where we had been invited to dinner. Our host lived in a simple house perched high above the main village, and the narrow room in which we ate was kept warm by an open log fire. For dinner we had a whole lamb stuffed with oregano. The herb grows wild all around the village and the local people gather huge bundles of it. They hang it out to dry, then remove the leaves and steep them in hot water to use for stuffing the lamb. It was perfectly delicious, and not as overpoweringly strong as one would imagine. Because such a large amount of oregano is difficult to obtain, I have worked out a recipe using spinach leaves well-laced with this pungent herb.

2 kg (4 lb) leg of lamb, boned
500 g (1 lb) spinach, lightly boiled, strained and chopped
3 tbsp oregano, steeped in boiling water for 5 minutes and drained
1 egg
2 tbsp olive oil
Salt and freshly ground black pepper

First prepare the stuffing. Combine the spinach, oregano, egg, olive oil, salt and pepper, and mix well. Lay the lamb out flat and spread the stuffing over it. Roll, shape and tie the meat; take care to enclose all the stuffing. Place in an oiled roasting pan and season with salt and pepper. Roast in an oven preheated to 190°C (375°F) for one and a half to two hours, or until tender.

Serves 4 to 6

Lamb Fricassé

Αρνί Φρικασέ

One of the true highlights of Greek cuisine! Curly endive is more tasty than romaine lettuce, and is not as bitter. The dish is quite easy to prepare, and the result is impressive.

1.5 kg (3 lb) lamb shoulder or leg, cut into serving pieces
1 kg (2 lb) curly endive or romaine lettuce, coarsely sliced
8 green onions, finely chopped
50 g (1 cup) finely chopped dill
30 g (2 tbsp) butter
¼ liter (1 cup) water
Salt and freshly ground black pepper
3 eggs, beaten until foamy
1 lemon, juice strained
Croutons for garnishing

Put the lamb, endive or lettuce, onions, dill, butter and water in a large flameproof casserole. Season with salt and pepper. Cover the casserole and bring slowly to the boil. Simmer for one hour, until the meat is tender and only about ¼ liter (1 cup) of liquid remains. Remove the casserole from the heat.

Beat the lemon juice into the eggs and pour the mixture over the meat while shaking the casserole vigorously. Reheat slowly without covering or boiling. Serve immediately with plain rice, garnished with croutons.

Variation: Substitute artichoke hearts for endive or romaine lettuce, and increase the water to ½ liter (2 cups).

Serves 6 to 8

Pork with Celery or Celeriac

Χοιρινό με Σέλινο

Greek celery differs from that which is normally available in the United States or Europe. Although it more closely resembles parsley in size and shape, the flavor is quite the same as our larger celery.

500 g (1 lb) boneless pork, preferably shoulder or neck end,
trimmed and cut in serving pieces
1 kg (2 lb) celery or celeriac with leaves, coarsely chopped
into bite-sized pieces
2 medium-sized onions, finely sliced
1 large carrot, thinly sliced
2 tbsp olive oil
Salt and freshly ground black pepper
1 egg
1 lemon, juice only
1 tbsp cornstarch (cornflour)
3 tbsp water

First parboil the celery (or celeriac) for 10 minutes. Strain, discard the water, and set the celery aside.

Dry the pork well. In a large flameproof casserole, sauté the pork, onions and carrot together in the olive oil for 10 minutes. Add the parboiled celery, season with salt and pepper, and cover with hot water. Simmer for about 1 hour, or until the meat is tender.

Now prepare the egg and lemon sauce. In a bowl, dissolve the cornstarch in the water; slowly add to it the casserole liquid, stirring constantly. Transfer the mixture to a saucepan and heat slowly, stirring constantly, until the sauce thickens.

Next beat the egg until light and frothy, then slowly add the lemon juice to it. Stir this mixture into the sauce.

Transfer the meat and celery to a serving dish and pour the sauce over. Serve with plain pilaf or parslied new potatoes.

Serves 6

Pork Chops Crassáta

Χοιρινές Μπριζόλες Κρασάτες

A simple but different treatment for pork chops.

4 loin pork chops
½ liter (2 cups) water
15 g (1 tbsp) butter
¼ liter (1 cup) dry red wine
Salt and freshly ground black pepper
2 tsp oregano

In a covered frying pan, simmer the pork chops in the water, turning occasionally, until the water evaporates and the chops are tender, about 25 minutes. Add the butter and wine to the frying pan. Continue cooking, uncovered, until the chops are browned on both sides, about 20 minutes more.

Season with salt, pepper and oregano and serve with mashed potatoes.

Serves 4

Souvlákia

Σουβλάκια

A favorite sidewalk snack in most of mainland Greece and the islands. The quality of meat used greatly affects the end result.

500 g (1 lb) leg of pork, cut in 2 cm (1 in) cubes
3 tbsp olive oil
1 lemon, juice strained
1 tsp oregano
2 green peppers, seeded and cut into 3 cm (1 in) squares
2 medium-sized tomatoes, cut in eighths
8 to 12 bay leaves
1 onion, very finely sliced
Salt and freshly ground black pepper
Cayenne pepper
Thick Greek pita bread
Tzatzíki (page 14)

Make a marinade of the olive oil, lemon juice and oregano. Let the pork marinate for at least one hour. Remove the meat from the marinade and dry the pieces with paper towels.

Using bamboo or metal skewers, alternate about six cubes of meat with pieces of green pepper, tomato and bay leaves for each souvláki. Barbeque or grill the souvlákia for 10 to 15 minutes, occasionally turning and brushing with olive oil and lemon juice.

Arrange the souvlákia on a serving dish, garnish with the sliced onion and sprinkle with salt, cayenne and black pepper and oregano. Serve with warmed píta bread and tzatzíki.

Variation: Remove the souvlákia from the skewers and serve rolled in warmed pita bread, well seasoned and topped with tzatzíki and onion. Tender beef, veal or lamb cubes may be substituted for the pork.

Serves 4

Spetsofái

Σπετζοφάι

This sausage dish is the specialty of the region of Mount Pilion, and is often the only meat available in mountain tavérnas during the winter months. Local people still make their own sausages.

250 g (½ lb) spicy sausages, sliced 1 cm (½ in) thick
8 green peppers, seeded and cut into 1 cm (½ in) strips
3 tbsp olive oil
3 medium-sized tomatoes, halved, seeded and grated, skins discarded
Salt and freshly ground black pepper
¼ tsp sugar

Sauté the peppers in 2 tbsp of the olive oil until they brown slightly. Add the tomatoes, and season with salt, pepper and sugar. Simmer for 20 to 25 minutes or until the sauce thickens. In another pan, sauté the sausages lightly in the remaining oil. Add them to the green peppers and simmer together for five minutes. Serve hot.

Serves 4

Rabbit Stifádo

Κουνέλι Στιφάδο

Stifádo is the most popular way of preparing rabbit, and by far the most delicious way to eat it.

1 large rabbit, cut into serving pieces
1.5 kg (3 lb) small onions, peeled and left whole
18 cl (3/4 cup) olive oil
3 cloves
2 bay leaves
¼ liter (1 cup) dry white wine
3 medium-sized tomatoes, halved, seeded and grated,
skins discarded
Marinade
¼ liter (1 cup) wine vinegar
¾ liter (3 cups) water
1 onion, quartered
1 carrot, sliced
2 celery sticks
3 to 4 cloves
1 tsp peppercorns
2 bay leaves

Combine the marinade ingredients in a glass or enamel bowl. Make sure all pieces are covered, and marinate the rabbit in the refrigerator over-night.

The next day, remove the rabbit and dry the pieces well. Sauté them in 4 tbsp of olive oil until browned. Set aside. In the same oil, sauté the onions and set aside.

Heat the remaining olive oil in a large casserole and add the rabbit, onions, cloves and bay leaves. Heat well, then add the wine and tomatoes. Partially cover and simmer for 30 minutes, or until the rabbit is tender. Serve with mashed potatoes.

Serves 4 to 6

Lamb with Eggplant

Αρνί με Μελιτζάνες

1 kg (2 lb) loin or leg of lamb, fat removed, cut into serving pieces
1 kg (2 lb) eggplant, unpeeled, cut in 5 cm (2 in) chunks
Olive oil for sautéing
1 medium-sized onion, finely sliced
3 medium-sized tomatoes, halved, seeded and grated,
skins discarded
1 garlic clove, crushed
2 tbsp finely chopped parsley
¼ tsp sugar
Salt and freshly ground black pepper
3 eggs, beaten
125 g (1 cup) grated kephalotýri or Parmesan cheese

Heat 2 tbsp of olive oil in a large flameproof casserole and sauté the lamb and onion for five minutes. Add the tomatoes and season with the garlic, parsley, sugar, salt and pepper. Simmer for 30 minutes, or until the meat is tender.

Heat 2 cm (1 in) of olive oil in a frying pan and sauté the eggplant until lightly browned. Drain well on paper towels.

Add the eggplant to the meat, cover and bake in an oven preheated to 190°C (375°F) for 30 minutes.

Beat the eggs and cheese together, pour them over the casserole and bake uncovered 10 minutes more, until set.

Serves 6 to 8

Rabbit Riganáto

Κουνέλι Ριγανάτο

1 large rabbit, cut in serving pieces
¼ liter (1 cup) wine vinegar
4 bay leaves
Salt and freshly ground black pepper
12 cl (½ cup) olive oil
¼ liter (1 cup) dry white wine
3 medium-sized tomatoes, halved, seeded and grated,
skins discarded
4 garlic cloves, finely chopped
1 cinnamon stick
½ tsp nutmeg
½ tsp sugar
125 g (4 oz) cubed ladotýri, pecorino or Parmesan cheese
2 tsp oregano

In a glass or enamel bowl, marinate the rabbit in the vinegar and bay leaves overnight in the refrigerator.

The next day, dry the rabbit well and sprinkle it with salt and pepper. In a frying pan, heat the olive oil until it smokes, and brown the rabbit on all sides. Remove the rabbit from the pan.

Transfer the oil to a flameproof casserole. Add the wine, tomatoes, garlic, cinnamon, nutmeg, sugar, salt and pepper. Simmer for 10 minutes. Add the rabbit and simmer slowly for one hour, or until the rabbit is tender. Stir in the cheese and oregano. Serve with fresh bread and wine.

Serves 4 to 6

Desserts, Cakes & Pastries

Halvá

Σπιτικός Χαλβάς

Halvá is the traditional dessert to serve during the fasting period of Lent. This recipe is for halvá spitikó, "homemade halvá". Commercially prepared halvá is made from a rich paste of ground sesame seeds, nuts and honey, and is eaten throughout the Middle East.

300 g (2 cups) semolina (cream of wheat), preferably
medium ground
¼ liter (1 cup) olive oil, or half oil and half butter
150 g (1 cup) blanched almonds, or half almonds and half pine nuts
400 g (2 cups) sugar
1 liter (4 cups) water, or 3 parts water and 1 part milk
2 cinnamon sticks
Icing sugar and ground cinnamon

Heat the oil (or oil and butter) in a saucepan and stirring constantly, sauté the almonds until golden. Reserve some nuts for decoration. Add the semolina to the remaining nuts in the saucepan, and cook and stir until it acquires a rich brown colour.

In another saucepan, combine the sugar, water and sticks of cinnamon; simmer them for five minutes, stirring to dissolve the sugar. Remove the cinnamon sticks and carefully pour the sugar liquid into the semolina. (If using, milk, add it now). Stirring constantly, simmer gently, until the semolina begins to leave the sides of the saucepan. Remove from the heat. Cover the saucepan with a cloth and lid, and let the mixture rest for 30 minutes.

Rinse out a ring mold with cold water, press the halvá into it, then turn it out onto a serving dish. Decorate with the reserved nuts and sprinkle with cinnamon and icing sugar.

Serves 8 to 10

Pastaflóra

Πασταφλόρα

450 g (3 cups) flour
2 tsp baking powder
225 g (8 oz) butter
100 g (½ cup) sugar
1 egg, beaten
6 cl (¼ cup) brandy or sherry
4 tbsp (¼ cup) apricot or strawberry jam
Blanched almonds and candied fruit (optional)

Sift together the flour and baking powder. In another bowl, cream the butter and sugar together, add the egg and mix well. Add the flour and brandy and mix again.

Roll out the pastry on a floured board to a thickness of 1 cm (½ in). Line a 24 cm (10 in) quiche dish with the pastry. Spread the jam over it and trim away the excess. Reroll the remaining pastry, cut it into strips, and with them make a lattice pattern on top of the jam. You may decorate the pastaflóra with almonds and candied fruit.

Bake in an oven preheated to 190°C (375°F) for 35 minutes, or until the pastaflóra is golden brown. Cool and cut in wedges.

Serves 8

Sýros Rice Pies

Συριανά Ρυζομπουρέκια

125 g (1 cup) short grain rice, boiled and strained
50 g (¼ cup) sugar
½ tsp nutmeg
1 tsp cinnamon
500 g (1 lb) phýllo pastry
¼ liter (1 cup) oil for frying
200 g (½ cup) honey

Combine the rice, sugar, nutmeg and cinnamon. Before unrolling the
phýllo, cut it into sections 5 cm (2 in) wide.

Unroll only one section at a time, and carefully separate the layers. Put a
teaspoon of the rice mixture on the corner of each strip and fold the
corner over to form a triangle (See page 54). Continue to fold the pastry
up as a triangle, using the whole strip. Fry the pies gently in hot oil until
golden brown, and drain well on paper towels. Arrange the pies on a
serving dish and drizzle the honey over them. Serve warm.

Makes about 24 small pies

Custard Cream Pie

Γαλακτομπούρεκο

Syrup
700 g (3½ cups) sugar
60 cl (2½ cups) water
Custard
1.75 liters (7 cups) milk
1 tsp grated lemon peel
8 eggs
500 g (2½ cups) sugar
150 g (1 cup) fine semolina (cream of wheat)
1 tsp vanilla extract
30 g (2 tbsp) butter
Pastry
500 g (1 lb) phýllo pastry
175 g (6 oz) butter, melted

To prepare the syrup, boil the sugar and water together for 20 minutes.
Let cool.

Now make the custard. In a large saucepan, heat the milk and lemon
peel until just lukewarm. Beat the eggs with the sugar until fluffly, then
pour them into the milk, stirring constantly. Add the semolina quickly,
and continuing to stir, cook without boiling until the custard thickens.
Stir in the vanilla and butter and set aside to cool.

Line a shallow baking tin, 24 by 36 cm (10 by 14 in), with 4 sheets of
phyllo, brushing each sheet liberally with melted butter. Pour over the
cooled custard and top with 5 sheets of phýllo, again brushing each
sheet with melted butter.

Carefully tuck any overhanging sheets of pastry under the pie and make
a few slits on top for steam to escape as the pie cooks. Bake in an oven
preheated to 190°C (375°F) for 25 minutes, or until browned. Remove
from the oven and pour the cool syrup over the pie. Cut into squares
while still warm.

Makes 15 servings

Baklavá

Μπακλαβάς

As moussaká is often one's introduction to savoury Greek cooking, baklavá is generally the first Greek sweet one encounters. The same prepackaged phýllo pastry that we use for so many pítas is soaked in a sugar/honey syrup that changes its character entirely. Be sure to keep the unused phýllo covered with a damp tea towel so that it doesn't dry out while you prepare the layers.

Pastry
500 g (1 lb) phýllo pastry
175 g (6 oz) unsalted butter, melted
Filling
450 g (3 cups) almonds, blanched and roughly chopped
1½ tbsp sugar
Syrup
400 g (2 cups) sugar
400 g (1 cup) honey, best possible quality
¼ liter (1 cup) water
2 tbsp rose water, optional
1 tbsp lemon juice

Line a 24 by 36 cm (10 by 14 in) baking tin with 4 sheets of phýllo pastry, brushing each sheet liberally with melted butter.
Combine the almonds and sugar, and sprinkle a third of the mixture over the phýllo. Place two sheets of phýllo on top, brushing each sheet with melted butter; sprinkle with another third of the almonds. Repeat these layers again, then top with two more sheets of phýllo, again brushing each sheet liberally with the melted butter.
Trim the excess phýllo to 2 cm (1 in) and fold it over to form an edging. Pour over any remaining butter and score the top layers of the baklavá into diamond shapes. Bake in an oven preheated to 190°C (375°F) for 35 minutes. Remove from the oven and leave to cool.
Boil the syrup ingredients together for 20 minutes and pour over the cooled baklavá. Follow the scoring to cut into serving pieces.
Variation: Walnuts may be substituted for almonds, cinnamon may be added to the nut mixture, or slices of lemon peel may be added to the syrup.
Makes 15 to 20 servings

Sfoliáta Sýros

Συριανή Σφολιάτα

Pastry
50 g (3 tbsp) butter
150 g (1 cup) flour
25 g (2 tbsp) sugar
1 egg, lightly beaten
Water
Filling
200 g (⅔ cup) apricot jam
5 eggs
100 g (½ cup) sugar
250 g (8 oz) ground roasted almonds
Topping
5 sheets phýllo pastry
100 g (3 oz) melted butter
Syrup
400 g (2 cups) sugar
80 cl (3½ cups) water

First make the pastry. Cut (or rub) the butter into the flour. Add the sugar and egg. Roll out the dough, and with it line the bottom of a 30 cm (12 in) baking tin. Spread the apricot jam over the pastry.

To prepare the filling, beat the eggs, sugar and almonds together and spread the mixture over the jam. Cover all with the phýllo pastry sheets, brushing each sheet liberally with melted butter. Score the phýllo into square serving pieces.

Bake in an oven preheated to 190°C (375°F) for 35 to 40 minutes. Meanwhile, boil the syrup ingredients together for 10 minutes. When the sfoliáta has cooled, pour the hot syrup over it. Cut into serving pieces along the scored lines.

Serves 12

Cinnamon Nut Ring

Κένκ Κανέλλας

This is an easy-to-prepare cake to serve with coffee.

225 g (8 oz) butter
400 g (2 cups) sugar
5 eggs
75 g (½ cup) finely chopped roasted almonds
75 g (½ cup) finely chopped roasted walnuts
450 g (3 cups) flour
3 tsp baking powder
2 tsp cinnamon
¼ liter (1 cup) milk

Cream the butter and sugar together. Add the eggs one at a time. Fold in the nuts. Sift together the flour, baking powder, and cinnamon. Add them to the mixture alternately with the milk.

Pour into a well buttered and floured 25 cm (10 in) tube pan or fluted cake tin. Bake in an oven preheated to 175°C (350°F) for 45 minutes, or until a toothpick inserted in the cake comes out clean. Cool on a rack for 10 minutes, then turn out of the pan.

Serves 12

Walnut Cake

Καρυδόπιτα

Karidópita, as it is known in Greece, is a rich and unusual dessert.

225 g (8 oz) butter
400 g (2 cups) sugar
7 egg yolks
150 g (1 cup) walnuts, chopped
1 lemon rind, grated
300 g (2 cups) flour
5 tsp baking powder
½ tsp cinnamon
7 egg whites, beaten until stiff
Syrup
300 g (1½ cups) sugar
½ liter (2 cups) water

Beat the butter and sugar together until light and frothy. Add the egg yolks one at a time, beating well. Stir in the walnuts and lemon rind. In another bowl, sift together the flour, baking powder and cinnamon. Stir this mixture into the butter and sugar. Gently fold in the egg whites. Pour the batter into a buttered 25 cm (10 in) cake pan. Bake in a moderate oven preheated to 190°C (375°F) for about 40 minutes, or until a toothpick inserted in the cake comes out clean. Let cool.

Meanwhile prepare the syrup by boiling the sugar and water together for 10 minutes. When the cake has cooled, pour the hot syrup over it. Cool again before serving.

Makes one 25 cm (10 in) cake

Ravaní

Ραβανί

300 g (2 cups) fine semolina (cream of wheat)
225 g (8 oz) butter
100 g (½ cup) sugar
5 eggs
150 g (1 cup) flour
3 tsp baking powder
¼ tsp vanilla extract
1 tsp grated lemon rind
Syrup
400 g (2 cups) sugar
85 cl (3½ cups) water

Cream the butter and sugar together until fluffy. Add the eggs one at a time, beating well after each addition. Sift together the flour, baking powder and semolina. Add the sifted ingredients, the vanilla, and the lemon rind to the creamed mixture. Stir well; the batter will be rather thick.

Spread the batter evenly into a 30 cm (12 in) round buttered baking tin, and bake in an oven preheated to 190°C (375°F) for one hour, or until a toothpick inserted in the center of the cake comes out clean. Let cool in the pan.

Meanwhile prepare the syrup by boiling the sugar and water together for 10 minutes. Pour half of the syrup over the cooled cake. Cut into serving squares, then pour the remaining syrup over. You may serve the ravaní topped with a spoonful of whipped cream.

Serves 12

Yogurt Cake

Γιαουρτόπιτα

225 g (8 oz) butter
400 g (2 cups) sugar
4 eggs
1 orange, rind grated
350 g (1½ cups) yogurt
450 g (3 cups) flour
4 tsp baking powder
¼ tsp salt
2 tbsp brandy
1 tsp vanilla extract
75 g (½ cup) currants
75 g (½ cup) roughly chopped roasted almonds

Cream the butter and sugar together until fluffy. Add the eggs, orange rind and yogurt, and beat.

Sift together the flour, baking powder and salt. Add half of the flour to the creamed mixture and beat; then add the brandy and vanilla and beat again. Add the remaining flour and beat until just smooth. Stir in the currants and almonds.

Transfer to a round buttered baking tin, 30 cm (12 in) in diameter, or a 24 by 30 cm (9 by 12 in) oblong tin. Bake in an oven preheated to 190°C (375°F) for one hour, or until a toothpick inserted in the center of the cake comes out clean.

Serves 12

Naki's Mocha Torte

Τούρτα Μόκα

This torte is easy to prepare and particularly attractive.

36 ladyfingers (sponge fingers)
350 g (12 oz) butter at room temperature
5 eggs
6 tbsp confectioners' (icing) sugar
1 tsp instant coffee diluted in 1 tbsp water
3 tbsp fresh cream (optional)
35 cl (1½ cups) milk
8 cl (⅓ cup) brandy
150 g (1 cup) almonds, blanched, roasted and chopped

Cream the butter until light and fluffy. Add the eggs, sugar, instant coffee and cream, and beat again until fluffy. Set aside.

Combine the milk and brandy. Quickly dip each ladyfinger into this mixture.

Arrange a third of the ladyfingers in a layer on an oblong serving platter. Spread with ¼ of the coffee-cream mixture. Add another layer of ladyfingers and coffee-cream, then top with remaining ladyfingers. Cover the sides and top with the remaining coffee-cream and refrigerate overnight. Sprinkle the chopped almonds over all before serving.

Serves 12

Chocolate Roll

Κορμός Σοκολάτα

This is an unusual cake as it contains no flour. The combination of whipped cream and chocolate is a delight.

7 eggs
400 g (2 cups) sugar
100 g (1 cup) cocoa
½ liter (2 cups) whipped cream
Icing sugar

Butter a jelly or Swiss roll tin, 24 by 36 by 2 cm (10 by 15 by 1 in), and line it with buttered waxed (greaseproof) paper. Beat the egg yolks with the sugar until creamy. Add the cocoa and stir well.

Beat the egg whites until stiff, then fold them gently into the cocoa mixture. Spoon the mixture into the prepared tin, smoothing it with a knife to evenly cover the pan. Bake in an oven preheated to 190°C (375°F) for 20 minutes, or until well risen and springy.

Cool slightly, then turn out onto a sheet of waxed paper sprinkled with 2 tbsp of sugar. Remove the lining paper from the bottom of the cake and trim off any hard edges. Roll up the warm cake and waxed paper together and let cool completely.

Carefully unroll and remove waxed paper. Spread the cake with the whipped cream to within 1 cm (½ in) of the edges. Starting at the short side, roll up the cake. Sprinkle it with icing sugar or cover with more whipped cream.

Serves 8

ASSEMBLING THE ROLL

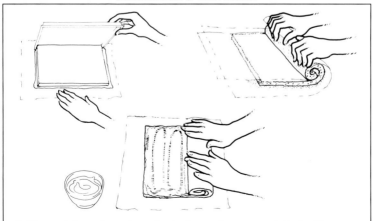

1. Turn out the cake onto a sheet of waxed paper sprinkled with sugar. Trim off hard edges. **2.** Roll up cake and waxed paper together, without filling. Let cool. **3.** Unroll and spread the cake with whipped cream to within 1 cm (½ in) of the edges. Reroll.

Coconut Cake

Τούρτα με Καρύδα

100 g (1 cup) icing sugar
225 g (8 oz) butter, melted
6 egg yolks
225 g (1½ cups) flour
2 tsp baking powder
250 g (1½ cups) dessicated coconut
12 cl (½ cup) milk
6 egg whites, beaten until stiff
75 g (½ cup) blanched, toasted and chopped almonds
24 cl (1 cup) whipped cream (optional)
Syrup
100 g (½ cup) sugar
½ liter (2 cups) water
1 tbsp lemon juice

Beat the icing sugar and butter together until pale. Add the egg yolks and beat well.
In another bowl, sift together the flour and baking powder; stir in the coconut. Add the flour mixture and milk alternately to the butter mixture, beating after each addition. Gently fold in the beaten egg whites.
Pour the batter into a generously buttered cake ring, of approximately 25 cm (10 in) diameter. Bake in an oven preheated to 190°C (375°F) for 35 to 40 minutes. Turn the cake out onto a plate.
To prepare the syrup, boil the ingredients together for 10 minutes. Pour over the cooled cake, and let the cake cool again. If you are using the whipped cream, spread it over the cake before topping it with toasted almonds.
Makes one 25 cm (10 in) ring cake

Chestnut Cake

Κέηκ από Κάστανα

This is a wickedly rich plethora of chestnuts, eggs and cream.

500 g (1 lb) sweetened chestnut purée, fresh or tinned
5 eggs, separated
½ tsp vanilla extract
½ liter (2 cups) whipped cream
Marrons glacés to decorate

Beat the egg yolks well and add them to the chestnut purée.
Beat the egg whites until stiff and fold them carefully into the chestnut mixture; flavor with the vanilla.
Pour into a round buttered baking tin and bake in a moderate oven, preheated to 190°C (375°F) for 45 minutes, or until a toothpick inserted in the center of the cake comes out clean. Let cool for 10 minutes before turning the cake out onto a plate to cool completely. Cover with the whipped cream and decorate with the marrons glacés.
Serves 10

Chestnut Delight

Τούρτα από Κάστανα

The less ambitious cook may want to buy praline already prepared, rather than make it at home.

1 kg (2 lbs) chestnuts, boiled and cleaned
250 g (½ lb) ladyfingers (sponge fingers)
150 g (⅔ cup) sugar
1 tbsp cocoa
75 cl (3 cups) milk
12 cl (½ cup) brandy
Topping
150 g (5 oz) butter
100 g (1 cup) icing sugar
4 egg yolks
1 tbsp Grand Marnier
Praline
200 g (1⅔ cups) almonds, blanched and lightly roasted
200 g (1 cup) sugar
1 lemon, juice strained

First prepare the praline. Combine sugar and lemon juice in a saucepan and heat, stirring constantly, until the sugar melts. Boil until the mixture turns a golden color. Add the almonds and mix well.
Pour the mixture out on an oiled surface, preferably marble. When the almonds have cooled, coarsely chop them in a food processor or blender, or crush them in a mortar, and set aside.
Combine 50 cl (2 cups) of the milk with the brandy. Dip the ladyfingers in the mixture and arrange them in one layer on a large cake dish.
Mix together the chestnuts, sugar, cocoa and the remaining milk. Beat until the mixture becomes a thick purée. Spread this over the ladyfingers.
To prepare the topping, beat the sugar and butter together. Add the egg yolks and Grand Marnier and beat well. Spread the topping over the chestnut purée and sprinkle the praline over all.
Serves 10

Pastéli

Παστέλι

Pastéli, sesame honey bars, are a delicious and healthy sweet. They are always made for paniyíria, Greek church festivals, and are sold by vendors at street stalls.

600 g (1½ lbs) sesame seeds
450 g (1 lb) honey
2 tbsp finely chopped orange peel

Lightly brown the sesame seeds in a heavy frying pan, stirring constantly. Bring the honey to the boil in a saucepan and add the orange peel and the sesame seeds. Boil until a teaspoon of the mixture poured into a glass of cold water does not dissolve, but holds together.
Pour the mixture onto a marble slab or other surface covered with oiled waxed (greaseproof) paper and spread it into a square shape about 1 cm (½ in) thick. Cut into 4 by 8 cm (1½ by 3 in) bars. You may sprinkle the pastéli with hundreds and thousands.

Caramel Pudding

Πουτίγγα

This is a delicious sweet made in the Ionian islands. It is probably a culinary hybrid of the British and French occupations there, as it seems to be a combination of an English trifle and a French crème caramel.

125 g (¼ lb) ladyfingers (sponge fingers), cut in small pieces
125 g (¼ lb) mixed candied fruit, chopped
75 g (½ cup) almonds, blanched, toasted and coarsely chopped
4 eggs
½ liter (2¼ cups) warm milk
100 g (½ cup) sugar
¼ tsp vanilla extract
1 lemon, rind grated
Caramel
100 g (½ cup) sugar
12 cl (½ cup) water

First prepare the caramel. Boil the sugar and water together, stirring until the sugar melts. Leave the mixture to boil without stirring until it turns a rich brown color. Remove the caramel from heat.

Meanwhile, warm a 18 cm (7 in) round soufflé dish. When the caramel has cooled slightly, pour it into the dish and turn to coat the sides and bottom with the caramel.

Place one-third of the ladyfingers in the bottom of the soufflé dish. Sprinkle half of the candied fruit and a third of the almonds over. Make another layer of ladyfingers and sprinkle over the remaining candied fruit, and a third of the almonds. Top with the rest of the ladyfingers.

Beat the eggs, milk, sugar, vanilla and lemon rind together. Pour the mixture slowly over the ladyfingers so that all are evenly moistened.

Bake the pudding in a bain-marie for 50 minutes in an oven preheated to 190°C (375°F) or until a toothpick inserted in the pudding comes out clean. Cool in the soufflé dish, then turn out onto a large round platter. Decorate with the remaining almonds.

Serves 6 to 8

Orange Yogurt Ambrosia

Γιαούρτι Σακούλας με Πορτοκάλι

To make your own strained yogurt from the thinner American or English product, start with at least double the quantity called for in your recipe. Put the yogurt in a cheesecloth bag and strain it over the sink overnight. The water will drain off, leaving a yogurt so thick that you can almost cut it with a knife.

1 kg (2 lb) Greek strained yogurt
2 to 3 oranges, juice only
1 orange, rind grated, then peeled and sliced
400 g (1 cup) honey, or 200 g (1 cup) sugar
75 g (½ cup) chopped walnuts

Place the yogurt in a nylon sieve and let drain for two hours to remove excess liquid. Stir the orange juice, orange rind and honey (or sugar) slowly into the yogurt. Refrigerate for at least 1 hour.
Transfer the yogurt to a glass bowl, sprinkle with walnuts, garnish with the orange slices, and serve.
Serves 6 to 8

Yogurt Cheesecake

Γιαουρτόπιτα

This is a lovely light cheesecake, and practically dietetic compared to some richer cream cheese and egg versions.

450 g (2 cups) Greek strained yogurt
250 g (½ lb) graham crackers (digestive biscuits), crushed
125 g (½ cup) butter, melted
14 g (½ oz) powdered gelatine
6 cl (¼ cup) water
200 g (1 cup) sugar
2 lemons, rinds grated and juice strained

Blend or process the biscuits and butter together until the butter is absorbed. Press the mixture evenly into the bottom and sides of a 25 cm (10 in) flan tin and set aside.
In a small saucepan, soak the gelatine in the water for a few minutes. Heat and stir until the gelatine dissolves.
Beat together the yogurt, sugar, lemon juice and rind. Quickly stir in the gelatine. Pour the mixture over the graham cracker crust and refrigerate for at least four hours. Serve decorated with fresh fruit.
Serves 6 to 8

Greek Frozen Yogurt

Παγωτό Γιαούρτι

This recipe is best made in a electric ice cream maker. It is easily prepared, yet it is the most delicious and healthy ice cream I have ever tasted. Try using other fresh fruits as they are in season; each flavor is better than the next! Adjust the amount of brown sugar or honey used, according to the sweetness of the fruit and you own preference.

450 g (2 cups) Greek strained yogurt
250 g (½ lb) fresh apricots, pitted
4 tbsp light brown sugar or honey
1 tbsp orange juice
¼ tsp cinnamon (optional)

Process all the ingredients together in a blender or food processor, then follow the instructions that come with your ice cream maker for freezing. If not using an ice cream maker, freeze the fruit mixture closely covered with plastic wrap until it is half frozen. Remove from the freezer and beat or process well. Freeze again before serving.
Serves 4

Baked Fruit Salad

Φρουτοσαλάτα του Φούρνου

A new version of an old favorite, this dessert is as versatile as it is unexpected.

3 bananas, sliced
1 medium-sized pineapple, peeled, cored
and chopped
250 g (½ lb) dried Kalamáta figs, chopped
24 cl (1 cup) fresh orange juice
1 lemon, juice only
100 g (4 tbsp) Greek honey
12 cl (½ cup) brandy
Greek strained yogurt or fresh cream

Combine the fruit, juices, honey and brandy in an ovenproof dish. Leave them to marinate, covered, for about four hours.
Bake the fruit salad in an oven preheated to 190°C (375°F) for 45 minutes. Serve warm or cold, topped with strained yogurt or fresh cream.
Serves 6

Easter Cookies

Πασχαλινά Κουλούρια

Kouloúria, as they are called in Greek, are generally prepared at home for Easter morning breakfast. The rest of the year, almost every bakery prepares its own version of this very popular cookie.

225 g (8 oz) butter
300 g (1½ cups) sugar
1½ tsp cinnamon
1 tsp vanilla extract
5 eggs
500 g (4 cups) flour, or more if needed
2½ tsp baking powder
6 cl (¼ cup) brandy

Cream the butter and sugar together until light and fluffy. Add the cinnamon and vanilla, beat again, then add the eggs one at a time, beating after each addition.
Sift the flour and the baking powder together and add them alternately with the brandy to the butter and sugar mixture. The dough should be fairly soft. With your hands roll the dough out like a sausage, 1 cm (½ in) in diameter. Cut into 10 cm (4 in) lengths. Form them into various shapes: twists, rings or loveknots.
Put the cookies on a buttered baking sheet and bake in a moderate oven preheated to 190°C (375°F) until they are lightly browned, about 25 minutes.
Makes 60 to 70 cookies

Melomakárona

Μελομακάρονα

These are the companion cookies to kourabiédes, and are also generally piled high in a pyramid. Having been soaked in the honey/sugar syrup, they stay fresh for up to two weeks even without refrigeration.

70 cl (3 cups) olive oil
100 g (1 cup) icing sugar
½ tsp baking soda
24 cl (1 cup) orange juice
12 cl (½ cup) brandy
1 tsp ground cinnamon
1 tsp ground cloves
1 kg (8 cups) flour
3 tsp baking powder
150 g (1 cup) chopped walnuts
Syrup
200 g (1 cup) sugar
½ lit (2 cups) water
400 g (1 cup) honey

Beat the oil and sugar together. Dissolve the baking soda in the orange juice and add it to the oil-sugar mixture. Then add the brandy, cinnamon and cloves, mixing well.

Sift the flour and baking powder together, combine with the other ingredients and knead well. The dough should be soft.

Shape into oblong cookies about 7 cm (3 in) long. Bake them on an ungreased baking sheet for 15 to 20 minutes, in an oven preheated to 190°C (375°F). Remove from the oven when done and leave to cool.

Now prepare the syrup. Boil the sugar, water and honey together for 10 minutes. Carefully dip each cooled cookie briefly in the boiling syrup and place on a large platter. Sprinkle the cookies with the chopped walnuts and additional cinnamon.

Makes about 40 cookies

Christmas Cookies

Κουραμπιέδες

Kourabiédes, one of the two popular Christmas cookies, are almond flavored shortbreads covered with plenty of snow-like confectioners' sugar. Be careful not to inhale while eating!

450 g (1 lb) unsalted butter
600 g (5 cups) confectioners' (icing) sugar, sifted
1 tsp baking powder
18 cl (¾ cup) brandy
750 g (7½ cups) all purpose flour
150 g (1 cup) almonds, blanched, roasted and chopped

Cream the butter and ½ cup of sugar together until light and fluffy. Dissolve the baking powder in 12 cl (½ cup) of the brandy and add it to the mixture. Add 150 g (1 cup) of flour and the almonds, beating constantly. Add the rest of the flour slowly, still beating, until the dough is soft but not sticky.

Shape tablespoons of the mixture into 4 cm (2 in) balls or crescents. Flatten each one slightly as you arrange the cookies on a baking sheet. Bake them in a moderate oven preheated to 190°C (375°F), for 15 to 20 minutes; they should not brown on top. When done, transfer the cookies to a large dish, sprinkle them with the remaining brandy and sieve most of the remaining icing sugar over. Pile the cookies in a pyramid on a round serving plate and sieve over the rest of the icing sugar.

Makes about 50 cookies

Apple Delight

Μήλο Γλυκό

This is a very simple dessert, but refreshing and light after a rich meal. The flavor of the apple is delightful on its own, but if you like, add brandy, rum or your favorite liqueur to taste.

3 kg (6 lb) apples, peeled, quartered and cored
100 g (½ cup) sugar (or more, if the apples are tart)
2 tsp ground cinnamon
1 to 2 tbsp lemon juice
½ liter (2 cups) whipped cream
75 g (½ cup) almonds, blanched, roasted and chopped

In a heavy saucepan, simmer the apples and sugar together very slowly until soft and thick, about one hour. Mash the apples with a fork and let them cool. Stir in the cinnamon and the lemon juice.
Transfer the apples to a large glass bowl, top with the whipped cream and sprinkle with the almonds. Chill well before serving.
Serves 6

Stuffed Prunes

Γεμιστά Δαμάσκηνα

These are delicious, simple to prepare, but out of the ordinary.

24 large pitted prunes
6 cl (¼ cup) brandy
12 cl (½ cup) water
40 g (¼ cup) walnuts, finely chopped
2 tbsp honey
1 tsp lemon juice
4 tbsp whipped cream to garnish

Soak the prunes in brandy and water overnight. The next day, remove the prunes from the brandy mixture.
Combine the walnuts, honey and lemon juice. Stuff each prune with a teaspoon of the walnut mixture. Arrange them attractively on a serving dish, and top with a whirl of whipped cream.
Serves 6 to 8

Figs with Honey

Σύκα με Μέλι

Fig trees grow all over Greece, from the most unexpected corner in the heart of Athens, to within the walls of ancient ruins. The fruit is so plentiful that it often goes unpicked.

500 g (1 lb) dried figs
½ liter (2 cups) white wine
200 g (½ cup) honey
¼ liter (1 cup) thick yogurt or fresh cream

Soak the figs in the wine for one hour, then simmer them in it for 20 minutes. Add the honey and simmer five minutes more.
Chill and serve topped with yogurt or cream.
Serves 8

Stuffed Figs

Παστελαριές

Try these during the winter in front of the fire, with a glass of brandy in hand.

36 ripe figs
100 g (⅔ cup) chopped walnuts
100 g (⅔ cup) chopped almonds
100 g (⅔ cup) sesame seeds

Bake the figs in a 190°C (375°F) oven for 15 minutes. Remove them and slice in half lengthwise.
Combine the chopped walnuts, almonds and sesame seeds. Use this mixture to stuff the figs, and fit the halves together again.
Bake the figs another 15 minutes, then cool well on a rack. When completely cool, store in tins.
Makes 36 pieces

Quince Jam

Κυδώνι Μαρμελάδα

1.5 kg (3 lb) quinces, unpeeled, cored and chopped
½ lemon, juice only
1.5 kg (3 lb) sugar
¼ liter (1 cup) water

In a bowl, cover the quinces with cold water and the lemon juice.
Simmer together the sugar and ¼ liter (1 cup) water in a large saucepan, stirring until the sugar has dissolved.
Drain the quinces and add them to the sugar syrup. Skimming off any foam that forms, simmer for 1½ hours, or until the quinces are transparent and soft. Store in sterilized jars.
Makes 2.5 kg (5 lb) jam

Baked Quinces

Κυδώνια στον Φούρνο

2 kg (4 lb) quinces, washed, halved and cored
300 g (1½ cups) sugar
¼ liter (1 cup) brandy
½ liter (2 cups) water
2 cinnamon sticks
6 cloves

Arrange the quinces in a flameproof baking dish, skin side up. Pour the remaining ingredients over them.
Cover the dish with aluminium foil and bake for two hours at 150°C (300°F). If the quinces have not turned a rosy color by this time, remove the foil and continue baking until they have.
To serve, slice the quinces and serve cold in individual bowls, topped with whipped cream or yogurt.
Serves 8 to 10

Index

167

Cosmos Publishing Co., Inc.
262 Rivervale Road
River Vale, N.J. 07675-6252
Phone: 201-664-3494

"The Source for Greek Literature"
"Η Πηγή του Ελληνικού Βιβλίου"